MW01115731

شَرْحُ الأُصُولِ السِّتَّةِ

Copyright © 2023 Najeeb Muhammad

A Publication of Charlot Publishing LLC

ISBN: 979-8-218-35155-7

All rights reserved. This book or any portion thereof may not be reproduced, distributed, transmitted, or used in any other manner whatsoever without the express written permission of the author, except in the case of brief quotations embodied in critical reviews and certain other noncommercial uses permitted by copyright law.

Author: Najeeb ibn Yusuf al-Anjelesi or Najeeb Muhammad
E-mail: najeebalangelesi@gmail.com

Designed by ihsaandesign.com

A Detailed Commentary
on the work of an
Insightful Luminary

An Explanation of
Sheikh Abu Ali Muhammad At-Tamimi's
Al-Usul As-Sittah

By
Najeeb ibn Yusuf al-Anjelesi

Contents

Acknowledgements

It is not appropriate to commence acknowledgments without initially giving praise and thanks to Allah, Lord of all existence. Whatever a person accomplishes, whatever positive and praiseworthy characteristics a person possesses, all are favors that Allah bestows upon him and the favors Allah bestows upon man are abundant and innumerable. Additionally, Allah can bestow upon a person a desire to embark upon accomplishing a goal, and grant him with the ability to pursue it; however, if He doesn't will for it to come to fruition, it will never be. Thus the success is with Him and acknowledgment of that is necessary. Allah says, what is rendered into the English language as:

وَءَاتَىٰكُم مِّن كُلِّ مَا سَأَلْتُمُوهُ وَإِن تَعُدُّوا نِعْمَتَ ٱللَّهِ لَا تُحْصُوهَآ إِنَّ ٱلْإِنسَٰنَ لَظَلُومٌ كَفَّارٌ

And He gave you all of what you requested of Him, and if you were to count the favors of Allah you would not be able to enumerate them. Undoubtedly man is certainly oppressive and ungrateful. [Ibrahim: 34]

Imam Fakhruddin Ar-Razi said: "i.e. He gave you all of that as it relates to what you need. Neither your circumstance nor daily needs can be rectified without it (i.e. what He gives). Thus it is as if you all asked and requested from him by way of your circumstance (i.e. of being in need of such not necessarily with verbal expression)."

Imam al-Baghawi said: "He gave you things that you requested and even that which you didn't ask for."

Thus I say all praises are due to Allah who bestowed upon me the ability to write, the knowledge to convey, the wherewithal to stay focused on the goal, and Him allowing me to complete this work. Additionally, whatsoever is connected to what I just mentioned from His favors that are innumerable. Gratefulness to Allah is taught by our scholars to be; acknowledgement of Allah's blessing upon you, praising Him on account of it, and perseverance as relates to obedience to Him. I ask Allah to make me a thankful servant who acknowledges the good bestowed upon me, praises Him, and strives in obeying Him in accordance with my ability. In addition to the previously mentioned, I find it incumbent to cite the statement of our Prophet ﷺ when he said: "He does not thank Allah whosoever does not thank the people." This speech is self explanatory and necessary to highlight as I continue my acknowledgements.

As it relates to the creation of Allah, First; I want to express my thankfulness to Yusuf Muhammad, the head of the administration to the Compton masjid i.e. Masjid Ar-Rashid, who has held that position for well over two decades. Most notably and more importantly, he is also my father from whom I inherited many of his characteristics by Allah's permission. My father was a member of the NOI during the last end of Elijah Muhammad's life. He entered this organization while serving time for murder. After being released from prison he dedicated his time in pursuit of seeing the organization's goals come to fruition, him and others. He remained in that group until the death of its leader in 1975 resulting in Warithuddin Muhammad being appointed as its new leader. At this point, he and my mother entered into Islam, eventually married shortly thereafter, which eventually led to my birth in 1978.

Although my parents separated while I was very young, my father played a pivotal role in my life. Regrettably during my teenage years I fell into some of the filth the Los Angeles streets offered, despite my experiences in that regard whenever my father was present he did his utmost best to instill certain values that prevented me from falling into certain ills and vices that others my age were falling into. He helped shape my behavioral approach to varying scenarios and situations. Throughout my adult years I have sought from him vital advice relating to multiple issues and received beneficial responses. In fact, when Allah placed a curiosity within me for actually understanding the religion I professed but didn't practice, it was my father who aiding me in that regard. I ask Allah to reward him immensely, forgive him for his shortcomings and mistakes, and bless him with good in this life and in the hereafter.

Second; I want to express my thankfulness to my teacher, mentor, and friend; the former imam of Masjid al-Mumin in Los Angeles and former head of Islamic studies at Al Madinah school, Sheikh Abu Mujahid Fareed Abdullah, may Allah act mercifully with him. He had a very positive impact on me as relates to understanding and implementation of Islam. He was a man that wanted good for his students and that good was exemplified by how he served the community in a positive way. He encouraged me to take advantage of my time by seeking clarity of Allah's religion. Thus I sat in his classes faithfully, rarely missing any. Likewise, he encouraged me to seek knowledge abroad, and gave my personal instructions on what to study to further my understanding of Islamic related affairs. Sheikh Fareed was a luminary who benefitted multitudes of brothers and sisters from his efforts, not just from classes, but also from mentoring, counseling, advising, etc. His work in terms of raising people upon the Sunnah is unparalleled here in the US, in my humble opinion. May Allah reward him immensely for his efforts, forgive him for his shortcomings, and grant him paradise without reckoning.

Third, I thank the brother Faizaan Ahmed of Sunnah Sauga. Initially he asked me to conduct classes on the book *The Six Principles* and he wanted to arrange a workbook for the classes based on the notes taken. The workbook idea eventually led to the production of this book that is before the reader today by Allah's permission. Thus I thank him for the initial spark in bringing this goal to fruition. May Allah reward him.

Lastly, there are many brothers and callers whose efforts are praiseworthy
and noble. I ask Allah to reward all of our brothers in dawah immensely
and to forgive them for whatever shortcomings they have with them,
or for whatever mistakes they may fall into while attempting to call the
people to Allah's guidance. Finally, all praises are due to Allah alone and
may His lofty commendations be upon our Prophet Muhammad and his
family.

Preface

The work in front of you titled: *Detailed Commentary to the Work of an Insightful Luminary*, came about as a result of a weekly course I conducted online in 2020. The class was an explanation of the original manuscript to the work *The Six Principles* by Sheikh Muhammad ibn Abdul Wahhab At-Tamimi An-Najdi along with usage of several contemporary scholars' explanations to this book, notably the explanation of Sheikh Muhammad ibn Salih al-Uthaymin. Subsequent to completing the course the organizer at Sunnah Sauga wanted to make a workbook for the original manuscript (translated into English) based on the notes taken from the course. He presented his notes to me on the introduction to the book for review and I found that the notes in some instances were incomplete in illustrating the points mentioned—from the class—in their entirety, resulting in me taking on the task of arranging the workbook.

Subsequent to embarking upon arranging the workbook I realized that the classes and how they were arranged sufficed for that type of endeavor; however, arranging the benefits on paper for the purpose of being returned to in book form differs tremendously in its composition to a live class. Consequently, I decided that a workbook was not the direction I wanted to go, instead an actual book should be compiled especially since I could be more detailed in explanation on paper as opposed to a live class online. Thus I embarked on writing this book despite the varying distractions that arose throughout the years while trying to complete it. All praises are due to Allah alone who blessed me to complete it, and I hope it will be a source of benefit for me in this life and in the next, likewise I hope it will be a benefit to its reader, and Allah is the Grantor of success.

Najeeb ibn Yusuf ibn Walter Charlot Sr, al-Anjelesi

Sept 25, 2023

The Six Principles (Manuscript)

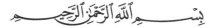

INTRODUCTION

Among the most remarkable of wonders and the greatest of signs indicating the ability of the Triumphant King are six principles that Allah elucidated with a blatantly obvious clarification for the general masses, being far above the suspicions of the naysayers/skeptics.

Thereafter—i.e. this clarification—many among the intellectuals of this world and the erudite thinkers among the descendants of Adam erred with regards to them except a small number among a minority.

FIRST PRINCIPLE

Ikhlas of the religion for Allah's sake alone without any—attributing of a—partner with him. Likewise a clarification of its opposite which is—deemed or dubbed—Shirk with Allah. In addition, the majority of the Quran, as relates to this fundamental, is a clarification from varying perspectives with utilization of speech that the most unintelligent of people comprehend.

Then there transpired, as pertains to the majority of the Islamic Nation, what transpired, as the Shaitan presented Ikhlas to them in the image of being prejudiced towards the righteous, and dereliction of their rights. Whereas Shirk with Allah, he presented it to them in the image of love for the righteous and emulation of them.

SECOND PRINCIPLE

Allah commands unity as pertains to religion and prohibits division therein. Hence He clarified this by way of a categorical explanation that the common folk comprehend. Likewise, He prohibited us from being like those—prior to us—who split and differed, consequently being destroyed. He adds clarity to this by what is reported, from the most remarkable of things,—found—within the sunnah. Thereafter, division within the fundamentals of the religion and its subsidiary issues became knowledge and comprehension of the religion, whereas unity in the religion became that which no one spoke about except a heretic or one mentally challenged.

THIRD PRINCIPLE

Undoubtedly the—mechanism—that completes unity is the hearing and obeying whomever is charged with authority over us, even though he may be an ethiopian slave. So Allah illustrated this with an adequate and prevalent clarification with varying perspectives among the types of elucidations both legislatively (as relates to Islam) and predictably predetermined. Thereafter this fundamental became unfamiliar with an abundance of those who claim knowledge, so how then is it enacted?

FOURTH PRINCIPLE

The elucidation of knowledge and the scholars, and Islamic jurisprudence and the Islamic Jurists, along with clarifying who resembles them yet is not from them. Allah clarifies this in the beginning portions of surah al baqara, from His statement,

$$\text{يَٰبَنِىٓ إِسۡرَٰٓءِيلَ ٱذۡكُرُواْ نِعۡمَتِىَ ٱلَّتِىٓ أَنۡعَمۡتُ عَلَيۡكُمۡ وَأَوۡفُواْ بِعَهۡدِىٓ أُوفِ بِعَهۡدِكُمۡ وَإِيَّٰىَ فَٱرۡهَبُونِ}$$

O descendants of Israel! Remember My favor I bestowed upon you and fulfill my covenant and I—in turn—will fulfill—the terms of—your covenant...

until His statement,

يَبَنِيٓ إِسۡرَٰٓءِيلَ ٱذۡكُرُواْ نِعۡمَتِيَ ٱلَّتِيٓ أَنۡعَمۡتُ عَلَيۡكُمۡ وَأَنِّي فَضَّلۡتُكُمۡ عَلَى ٱلۡعَٰلَمِينَ

O descendants of Israel! Remember My favor I bestowed upon you, and indeed I showed you preference over the rest of creation. (Al-Baqara:40-47)

He adds clarity—i.e. to this affair—by what the Sunnah made apparent as relates to clear, abundant, and manifest speech for the unintelligent commoner. Thereafter this became the strangest of things. Knowledge and Islamic Jurisprudence became innovation and misguidance, thus the best of what they possessed was a mixture of truth with falsehood. Consequently, knowledge that Allah made binding upon His creation and praised, no one uttered it except a heretic or one mentally challenged. Moreover whoever disapproved of, and held hostility towards it along with warning against and prohibiting it then he is the jurist and or scholar.

FIFTH PRINCIPLE

The clarification of Allah—The Glorified—concerning His awliyya, along with differentiation between them and those who resemble them from Allah's enemies, the hypocrites, and the immoral. Sufficient with regards to illustration of this is a verse in Ali-Imran (31) and it is His statement:

قُلۡ إِن كُنتُمۡ تُحِبُّونَ ٱللَّهَ فَٱتَّبِعُونِي يُحۡبِبۡكُمُ ٱللَّهُ

Say: "If you love Allah then follow me, consequently Allah will love you..."

Moreover the verse in Al-Maa'idah (54):

يَٰٓأَيُّهَا ٱلَّذِينَ ءَامَنُواْ مَن يَرۡتَدَّ مِنكُمۡ عَن دِينِهِۦ فَسَوۡفَ يَأۡتِي ٱللَّهُ بِقَوۡمٖ يُحِبُّهُمۡ وَيُحِبُّونَهُۥٓ

O you who believe! Whoever among you that turns away from his religion, will result in Allah coming with a people that He will love and they will love him...

Likewise the verse in Yunus (62-63):

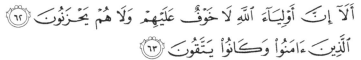

أَلَا إِنَّ أَوْلِيَاءَ ٱللَّهِ لَا خَوْفٌ عَلَيْهِمْ وَلَا هُمْ يَحْزَنُونَ ﴿٦٢﴾
ٱلَّذِينَ ءَامَنُوا۟ وَكَانُوا۟ يَتَّقُونَ ﴿٦٣﴾

Undoubtedly the awliyya of Allah shall not be overcome with fear nor shall they grieve. Those that believed and exemplify taqwa.

Thereafter this affair—with an abundance of those that feign knowledge among the guiders/mentors of the creation and the preservers of the Islamic Legislation—started to perceive—as relates to the awliyya—that it was necessary for them to abandon conformity to the messengers, therefore whoever followed the messengers was not among the awliyya. Furthermore (they perceived) that it was necessary—i.e. for the awliyya—to abandon jihad, hence whoever participated therein was not among them. Lastly (they also perceived) it to be necessary to abandon Al-Iman and Taqwa, so whoever committed himself to Al-Iman and taqwa was not among them

O our Lord! We ask You for pardon and protection, indeed You are the All Hearing of invocations.

SIXTH PRINCIPLE

Repelling the specious arguments devised by the Shaitan as relates to abandonment of the Quran and Sunnah, along with conformity towards differing opinions and desires. This specious argument is that the Quran and Sunnah are not known (i.e. comprehended) by anyone except a mujtahid mutlaq, who is described with traits that may not be found even with (figures such as) Abu Bakr and Umar.

Hence if a person does not match this criteria, then he is required to shun the Book and Sunnah compulsorily and there is neither doubt nor ambiguity in this regard (i.e. according to this false argument). In contrast to whomever seeks guidance from these two sources, as he—consequently is viewed as—a heretic or someone mentally challenged, on account of extreme difficulty in comprehending these two textual sources (per this argument/doubt).

SubhaanAllah wa bihamdihi; how many times has Allah elucidated (His) repelling of such accursed arguments from varying perspectives i.e. legislatively, by predetermination (aspects of such overtly predictable to man), by—keen observation of—the creation, and by—His devine—commandments; to the point that it reaches the boundaries of being known by necessity. Unfortunately an abundance of people are unaware.

إِنَّمَا تُنذِرُ مَنِ ٱتَّبَعَ ٱلذِّكۡرَ وَخَشِيَ ٱلرَّحۡمَٰنَ بِٱلۡغَيۡبِ فَبَشِّرۡهُ بِمَغۡفِرَةٍ وَأَجۡرٍ كَرِيمٍ ﴿١١﴾ إِنَّا نَحۡنُ نُحۡيِ ٱلۡمَوۡتَىٰ وَنَكۡتُبُ مَا قَدَّمُواْ وَءَاثَٰرَهُمۡۚ وَكُلَّ شَيۡءٍ أَحۡصَيۡنَٰهُ فِىٓ إِمَامٍ مُّبِينٍ ﴿١٢﴾ وَٱضۡرِبۡ لَهُم مَّثَلًا أَصۡحَٰبَ ٱلۡقَرۡيَةِ إِذۡ جَآءَهَا ٱلۡمُرۡسَلُونَ ﴿١٣﴾ إِذۡ أَرۡسَلۡنَآ إِلَيۡهِمُ ٱثۡنَيۡنِ فَكَذَّبُوهُمَا فَعَزَّزۡنَا بِثَالِثٍ فَقَالُوٓاْ إِنَّآ إِلَيۡكُم مُّرۡسَلُونَ ﴿١٤﴾ قَالُواْ مَآ أَنتُمۡ إِلَّا بَشَرٌ مِّثۡلُنَا وَمَآ أَنزَلَ ٱلرَّحۡمَٰنُ مِن شَيۡءٍ إِنۡ أَنتُمۡ إِلَّا تَكۡذِبُونَ ﴿١٥﴾ قَالُواْ رَبُّنَا يَعۡلَمُ إِنَّآ إِلَيۡكُمۡ لَمُرۡسَلُونَ ﴿١٦﴾ وَمَا عَلَيۡنَآ إِلَّا ٱلۡبَلَٰغُ ٱلۡمُبِينُ ﴿١٧﴾

Indeed the statement has been proven true against most of them, thus they will not believe. Certainly We have placed on their necks iron collars reaching their chins resulting in their heads being raised. And We placed a barrier before them and behind them, and We covered them so that they cannot see. It is the same to them regardless if you warn them or not, they will not believe. You can only (effectually) warn whomsoever conforms to the remembrance (i.e. the Quran), and knowingly fears the Infinitely Merciful (i.e. Allah) while unseen. Therefore give glad tidings of forgiveness and generous rewards to such a one (bearing the aforementioned praiseworthy traits). [Ya-Seen: 7-11]

In closing, all praise is due to Allah Lord of all that exists, and may He commend (in lofty gatherings) and grant peace upon our leader Muhammad, his family, and his companions until the day of resurrection.

Commentator's Introduction

Dear reader, the work in front of you is commentary to a manuscript rendered into English from the writings of the revivalist of Islamic monotheism and prophetic traditions of his time within the Arabian Peninsula, i.e. Sheikh Muhammad ibn Abdul Wahhab At-Tamimi An-Najdi, a specialist in Hanbali jurisprudence, a firmly grounded theologian, and prominent Sunni scholar of Islam. This work of his is in a summarized fashion from its introduction to the last principle mentioned. The Sheikh introduces the readers to religious facts and concepts derived directly from the text of the Quran and Sunnah; however, these concepts are devoid of intricate details needed for Muslims of contemporary times to fully comprehend. It should be noted that the Sheikh lived from 1703 to 1792, thus the concepts summarized within this manuscript may have been known generally to the Muslims of his locality at that time, and Allah knows best.

Nonetheless, this work was arranged for the purpose of elucidating the concepts found within the treatise of the Sheikh by providing Islamic technical definitions to important terms, explaining phrases and principles, providing the evidence for statements made, and quoting some of the prominent scholars of ancient and contemporary times with regards to the varying Islamic sciences relevant to each discussion. Thus, what is expected—by Allah's permission—is for the reader to gain a more detailed comprehension of the concepts presented within the treatise along with issues directly connected to them, especially considering the fact that some of these matters are from the fundamentals of the religion.

Likewise, some of these matters pertain to the safety and security of the Muslims within the Islamic community specifically and the Islamic Nation generally. The following is an outline of what each section will cover and what the reader is expected to learn, if Allah wills.

The Sheikh's introduction covers the meaning of the term *Bis-mil-llah-ir-Rahman-ir-Raheem*, what each word within this phrase means, and the overall meaning of the phrase. Additionally it clarifies the prophecies of the Messenger ﷺ as pertains to the condition of the Muslims in later times being of less quality in terms of righteousness than the believers in the first three generations. This, of course, is replete with textual evidence to support the statements and concepts initially presented by the Sheikh. The reader will learn and understand these affairs in detail, by Allah's permission.

The first principle covers the topic of ikhlas which is normally translated as sincerity. The Islamic technical definition along with other related issues pertaining to ikhlas are detailed giving the reader a well rounded understanding of the subject. Likewise the term shirk normally translated as polytheism is defined and detailed. The reader will learn about its types, ruling, and the dangerous consequences that its perpetrator is threatened with. This is from the essential matters of the religion made binding upon every Muslim to know.

The second principle will touch on the command for unity and prohibition on disunity. This consists of several related subjects being detailed e.g., the intent of the rope of Allah, the varying types of differing and their rulings, and other affairs connected to unity and disunity. The reader should gain a firm understanding as to what unity in Islam is, and the means to achieve such. Moreover, he/she will learn about the prohibited differing found within the text and the means to quail such, along with learning the various types of differing not held to the same standard as that which is prohibited. Ultimately, the reader will be able to distinguish between these affairs, by Allah's permission.

The third principle pertains to hearing and obeying the Muslim leader appointed to the position of head of state or governance over a large body of Muslims. The reader will gain comprehension of the intent to "hear and obey" along with affairs directly connected to this issue. For example, the application of hearing and obeying, the ruling pertaining to the tyrannical leader, rebellion and its ruling, when rebellion is justifiable, and other similarly related issues. This is of paramount importance, especially in this day and time when many speak about this issue without well rounded knowledge as pertains to the issue or no knowledge at all, just emotionalism and zeal which—if followed—could lead to ruin.

The fourth principle tackles the issue of knowledge, its importance and virtue, and its carriers. Among other things, the reader will obtain clarity with regards to the knowledge praised within revelation, the rulings connected to learning it, how to recognize its carriers, how to identify blameworthy knowledge and the proper ruling applied to such, and other relevant affairs connected to this subject. Hopefully, by Allah's permission it will be a means to foster enthusiasm in pursuing acquisition of this knowledge, and Allah knows best.

The fifth principle deals with the allies and or beloved (awliyya) to Allah. The reader will understand how the text defines awliyya, their status with Allah, their two categories as derived from the text, their characteristics, the danger of holding hostility towards them, and other related matters directly connected to the subject. This will enable the reader to determine the clear frauds who apply this term to themselves or to their mashaayikh, yet they clearly have characteristics that oppose how the text determines who they may be. Likewise, it will instill enthusiasm within the reader to strive to be among Allah's awliyya, due to their qualities being defined, and on account of the incentives mentioned within the text as a promise to them.

The sixth principle encourages living in conformity to Allah's revelation i.e., the Quran and Sunnah, and discourages abandonment of it. The reader will learn the textual evidence for adherence to the revelation, its ruling, and the incentives mentioned within the text for doing such. It will foster a sense of urgency in complying with the text on account of understanding that adherence to the revelation is the only means to one's salvation in this life and in the Hereafter.

Although most of these affairs are commonly known within social circles of students of knowledge studying traditionally within masaajid, Islamic centers, or in Islamic universities; they are not commonly known to the common Muslims who don't sacrifice their time, wealth, and self to embark upon the path of seeking knowledge. As a result some, if not all of these affairs are understood without detail gained from the pursuit of knowledge. Likewise, in the states many masaajid do not have qualified teachers who themselves took the time to seek knowledge from qualified teachers and specialists of Islamic sciences. As a result, these affairs or aspects of them are misrepresented by unqualified callers and misunderstood by those who open their hearts to the speech of the unqualified.

Hence, it becomes incumbent for people like myself, with Allah's aid, to take advantage of the means that will lead to spreading this knowledge to as many Muslims as possible if Allah wills. Undoubtedly, this writing is from the varying means to circulate beneficial knowledge throughout the US specifically and the world generally. Thus, it is hoped that Allah places blessings in my effort and causes this work to be a source of benefit for the Muslims in the English speaking world by His permission.

Lastly, all praises are due to Allah alone, He Who has blessed me to complete this writing by His permission and assistance. He Who is the sole possessor of the dominion of the heavens and the earth, He Who is All-Capable of doing whatever He wills. May He send His peace and lofty commendations upon His Messenger Muhammad, his family, and his companions.

Najeeb ibn Yusuf al-Anjelesi
Nov 13, 2023

Author's Introduction

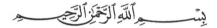

Among the most remarkable of wonders and the greatest of signs indicating the ability of the Triumphant King are six principles that Allah elucidated with a blatantly obvious clarification for the general masses, being far above the suspicions of the naysayers/skeptics.

Thereafter—i.e. this clarification—many among the intellectuals of this world and the erudite thinkers among the descendants of Adam erred with regards to them except a small number among a minority.

The author—may Allah reward him tremendously—established what is to be a recurring theme throughout his book, that being the message of Islam—during the time it was revealed—along with its goals and intent, being manifest and clear to its adherents i.e. to adults and children, men and women, freed and enslaved, rich and poor, Arab and non Arab, and intelligent and unintelligent. In contrast to generations that came later, as the people within these generations would misconstrue these overtly clear fundamentals and act in contradiction to them and to the way they were carried out at the time the revelation was revealed. The occurrence of this negative circumstance is not something that can neither be denied nor be difficult to comprehend, on the contrary this unfortunate situation was not only propesized—in clear and explicit terms—but is also witnessed by those whom Allah has given understanding as relates to these affairs.

The following statements of our Prophet ﷺ illustrate this unfortunate circumstance that the author alludes to in his introduction and throughout each specified principle:

> *The best of people is my generation, then those that are subsequent to them, then those that are subsequent to them. Thereafter there will come a people who will precede his testimony before his oath, and his oath before his testimony.*[32]

The virtues of the early generations are clearly highlighted within the Messenger's ﷺ speech, likewise the blameworthy characteristics found within latter generations are mentioned in unambiguous terms. Thus the difference in virtue, steadfastness, and righteousness are clearly defined. Al-Hafidh Ibn Hajr Al-Asqalaani said:

> The conclusion drawn from this narration is the equalization of virtues as pertains to the first three generations, even though they vary as relates to status, and this is applied in an overwhelming and plentiful sense. This is due to the fact that it is found with whomever comes after the companions, as pertains to the two succeeding generations, he who possesses these blameworthy aforementioned characteristics as well even though it may be minimal (throughout the broader community), in contrast to whoever comes after these three generations, as that -i.e. blameworthy traits- surely is plentiful and common amongst them.[33]

The Messenger of Allah said ﷺ:

> *The righteous will depart one after the other in succession, and the hufaalah (i.e useless part of a thing usually the last part or something inferior and low graded) similar to the useless portion of barely (i.e the*

---

32. Collected by Al-Bukhari: 2652, 3651 and Muslim: 2533. Upon the authority of Abdullah ibn Masud.

33. Fath-ul-Bari: 8/10.

husk) and or dates will remain, and Allah will have no concern for them.[34]

Within the statement of Allah's Messenger ﷺ there is an apparent description regarding the types of people that will exist in later times. His ﷺ speech elucidates the reality that they will be the most deplorable of people insomuch that the Most Merciful will have no concern for them. Al Hafidh ibn Hajr Al-Asqalaani said: "The intent of hufaalah is the inferior (low standard) among all things."[35]

The Messenger of Allah ﷺ said:

A time will come upon the people during which the patient one among them regarding his religion will be like the person grasping hot coals.[36]

Abul Ali Muhammad Abdur Rahman Al-Mubaarakfuri said:

At-Tayyibi stated "The meaning draws a resemblance to a person grasping hot coals being unable to be patient on account of the burning of his hand, similarly the religious person at that time will be unable to remain steadfast upon his religion due to the overwhelming amount of sinners and sinfulness along with the circulating of wicked behavior and weakness of faith."[37]

The Messenger of Allah ﷺ said: "There will come upon the people deceptive years wherein the liar -during that time- will be declared truthful and the truthful will be declared a liar. Likewise the deceiver will be declared trustworthy and the trustworthy will be declared and deceiver. Also the ruwaibidah will speak." And it was said "Who is the ruwaibidah?" To which he ﷺ replied "An insignificant man who speaks about widespread affairs (involving the Muslim nation).[38]

---

34. Collected by Al-Bukhari: 6434 and 4156. Narrated on the authority of Mirdaas Al-Aslami.

35. Fath-ul-Bari.

36. Collected by Tirmidhi: 2270. Declared authentic by Imam Al-Albani. Narrated on the authority of Anas ibn Malik.

37. Tuhfat-ul-Ahwadhi.

38. Collected by Ibn Majah: 4036, Ahmad, Al-Hakim, and others. Declared to be authentic

Abdul Ghani Al-Mujaddadi Ad-Dahlawi said: "Deceptive i.e. scheming and trickery. Attaching deception to years is from the perspective of allegory as the -real- intent are the people of these years."[39]

This interpretation is evident when examining the remainder of the narration and narrations similar to it in meaning. All point to the distinction between the early generations of Muslims, as pertains to their virtues on account of their comprehension and practical application, as opposed to those within generations succeeding them. These later generations, many within them adopted beliefs and practices foreign to that of their righteous predecessors consequently making them less in virtue, status, steadfastness upon guidance, and conformity to the truth. In fact some have differed with the practice of the early generations insomuch that it no longer aligns with traditional understanding and practice of Islam and is deemed to be outside of its boundaries.

In light of this scholars have encouraged extreme caution as relates to practical application of Islam, and have instructed people to thoroughly examine any belief and practice in order to ensure that it conforms with that which the early generation of Muslims practiced. The following are a few of these scholars' statements:

Umar ibn Abdil Aziz said: "Adopt the opinion that conforms to those who came before you, certainly they were more knowledgeable than you."[40]

Imam Ibrahim Al-Harbi said:

If a small person adopts the speech of Allah's Messenger ﷺ, the companions, and the taabi'een he -as a result- becomes senior, and if the senior sheikh adopts the statement of Abu Hanifah while abandoning the prophetic traditions he becomes small.[41]

Imam Al-Barbahari said:

Examine carefully all of whomever's speech you hear from the people of

---

by Imam Al-Albani. Narrated on the authority of Abu Huraira.

39. Injaah-ul-Haajah.

40. Fadl Ilm-us-Salaf, pg. 22.

41. Sharh Usool Itiqaad Ahlis Sunnah.

your particular time period and do not be hasty (i.e. in implementation of it). Do not enter into any of it until you first examine and ask, "Did anyone among the Prophet's ﷺ companions speak accordingly or anyone from the scholars?" If you stumble across a narration of theirs (either for or against the statement) then cling to it and do not exceed it for any reason. Likewise do not give preference to anything over it lest you slip into the fire.[42]

Imam Muhammad Nasruddin Al-Albani said: "The ideology of the Salaf (i.e. the companions) is safer, more knowledgeable, and wiser whereas the reverse (i.e. the generations after them) is not, in opposition to what is widespread among the contemporaries amid the scholars of rhetoric."[43]

We seek safety and security from Allah during these trying times that are replete with confusion.

BIS-MIL-LLAH-IR RAHMAN-IR-RAHEEM
The author commences his book with the phrase *"Bis-mil-llah-ir Rahman-ir-Raheem"* which is normally referred to as the *basmalah*. In order to fully understand the *basmalah* and its importance the subject must be divided into several separate—yet related—subjects, and they are as follows:

- What is the *basmalah*?
- What is the meaning of the *basmalah*?
- What is the difference between the *basmalah* and the *tasmiyyah*?
- Why is it important to pronounce the *basmalah*?

WHAT IS THE BASMALAH?
The basmalah is a *naht* (نَحْت) or a portmanteau word in English terms. It is a word that combines the form and meaning of two or more words, fusing and or blending them into one with reduced components. Thus the *basmalah* refers to the statement *bis-mil-llah-ir Rahman-ir-Raheem*;

---

42. Sharh-us-Sunnah.

43. Jaami Turath Al-Allamah Al-Albani, v. 1, pg. 193.

however, this sentence has been combined into one word i.e. *basmalah* which signifies the sentence uttered. The *basmalah* is not an anomaly within the Arabic Language, on the contrary examples of portmanteau words within the Arabic Language are available. Here are a few examples:

- The *hamdalah* (الحمدلة): referring to the statement *"Alhamdulillah"* i.e. all praises are due to Allah alone.
- The *Hawqalah* (الحوقلة): which refers to the statement *"La-Hawla wa la quwwata illa bil-lah"* i.e. there is neither might nor power except with Allah.
- The *Hay'ilah* (الحيعلة) which refers to the sentence *"Hayya alaas-Salaat"* i.e. hasten to the prayer.

Therefore if you find a person instructing another by saying, "You must pronounce the *basmalah*" in essence what he is saying is "You must say *bis-mil-llah-ir Rahman-ir-Raheem*" and Allah knows best.

WHAT IS THE MEANING OF THE BASMALAH?

An elucidation concerning the meaning of the *basmalah* necessitates delving into the meanings of each word within the sentence to acquire a complete understanding of its intent which in turn produces an unrivaled appreciation for what it entails.

**AL-BAA (الباء): this is the first portion of this sentence. The *Baa*—the portion pronounced *"bi"*—is equivalent to a proposition as it precedes a noun and expresses a relationship between it and another word. The word it precedes is normally translated—in the context of this sentence—as name, so the natural question is where is the other word that the *Baa* connects the word name with?

The renowned grammarian and scholar of fiqh jurisprudence Sheikh Muhammad ibn Salih Al Uthaymin answers this question. He states:

> The *baa* and the word subsequent to it being affected by it grammatically (the word translated as name) are directly related to an omitted verb suitably placed at the end (i.e. of the sentence). The missing syntactical

part implied -based on the context of the sentence- is *bis-mil-llah* I write.[44]

To fully comprehend the relationship between these two words and how the baa connects them, one must understand the meaning of *baa* in this sentence. Although *baa* has varying meanings depending on the context of the sentence, its usage here and what it indicates is clear and distinct. The former minister of Islamic Affairs for the Kingdom of Saudi Arabia Sheikh Salih Alish-Sheikh said: "The *baa* is for seeking assistance and reward stemming from the meaning of solicitation. Hence it is similar to him saying, "I write seeking assistance or soliciting reward with all of Allah's names."[45] This illustrates how the *baa* establishes the relationship between the word normally translated as name (i.e. name of Allah) and the omitted verb "I write" as solicitation is what links them. In other words, in order for the author to write he first seeks assistance with Allah's name to accomplish this endeavor.

AL-ISM (الاسم): this is the second word within this sentence normally translated as "name" as indicated previously. Although the word is in the singular form, it doesn't indicate particularization to a specified name. On the contrary it is unrestricted and envelopes all the names of Allah based on it being a definite word affixed (or possessed) by another definite word (i.e. the majestic expression Allah) linguistically within the language of the Arab. Sheikh Salih Al Fawzan said:

> His statement 'bis-mil-llah': ism is affixed and Allah is He to whom it's affixed. Its intent is all the names of Allah -glorified and exalted is He- on account that if a singular word is affixed (i.e. possessed) then it entails generality. Consequently his statement 'Bis-mil-llah' means with all of Allah's names I seek assistance...[46]

As for the remainder of words within the *basmalah*, they are names of the Lord of mankind. On account of this, it is imperative to understand a few

---

44. Sharh Al-Usul As-Sittah.

45. Sharh Al-Aqidat Al-Wasitiyah.

46. Sharh Lum'at Al-I'tiqad.

principles specific to His names prior to elaborating on their meanings, especially since knowledge of these names gives the worshiper a better understanding of He to Whom which his acts of worship are directed. Thus the following are some principles related to this subject that are of great importance to comprehend.

THE NAMES OF ALLAH ARE TITLES AND CHARACTERISTICS

Sheikh Muhammad ibn Salih Al Uthaymin said:

> They are titles in reference to them indicating the essence/self (i.e. of Allah), and they are also characteristics in reference to what they indicate from meanings. The first reference is (the names being) synonymous in indication of one (entity) being named and He is Allah. The second reference is that they vary as relates to their signification, each one from among them possessing a particular meaning. For instance; Al-Hayy, Al-Aleem, Al-Qadeer, As-Samee, Al-Baseer, Ar-Rahman, Ar-Raheem, Al-Aziz, Al-Hakeem, all are names as pertains to one entity designated and He is Allah. However, Al-Hayy has a specific meaning, As-Samee has a specific meaning, and Al-Baseer has a specific meaning.[47]

In layman's terms, the names are not meaningless. They are not merely titles or verbal expressions that indicate nothing, on the contrary they point to complete and perfect characteristics and attributes belonging to the carrier of these names i.e. Allah.

THE NAMES OF ALLAH ARE TAWQEEFIYYAH

Sheikh Muhammad ibn Salih Al Uthaymin said:

> In light of this, it is incumbent that learning them is restricted to what the Book and the Sunnah have brought, and to neither add nor subtract in that regard. This is due to the fact that the intellect is not capable of determining what the Exalted merits of names. Therefore it is binding to halt in that regard, being restricted to the text, due to His statements:
>
> **'And do not follow that of which you have no knowledge. Certainly**

---

47. Al-Qawaa'id Al-Mithla.

the hearing, sight, and heart; all of those a person will be questioned about.'[Al-Israa:37]

'Say: My Lord has only forbidden immorality -what is apparent and hidden of it-, sinfulness, transgression without due right, associating a partner with Allah of that which He has given no authority, and to say about Allah that which you know not.' [Al-A'raf: 33]

To name Him with that which He did not name Himself, or to deny what He named Himself is a serious offense as pertains to His right, as a result it is obligatory to possess ethical behavior as relates to this and restriction to what the text has brought (i.e. of names).[48]

ALLAH'S NAMES ARE SPECIFIED FOR HIM AND BEFITTING HIS MAJESTY

Sheikh Abdur Razzaq Al-Badr said:

Undoubtedly from the important principles and beneficial fundamentals as relates to the subject of comprehension of Allah's beautiful names is that they and His lofty attributes are specific for Him and befitting His majesty, perfection, and grandiose nature, just as He says: "And to Allah belongs the best of names so call on Him with them..."

Appending them to Him indicates their particularization to Him. On account of this, Allah names Himself with names and He names His attributes and these names are specific to Him as no one and or nothing shares anything with Him as pertains to them. There is no partner with Him concerning them, no duplicate, no equal, and no counterpart. In addition Allah -the blessed and exalted- designated some of His creation with names specific to them, i.e. appending it to them. Appending these names to them indicates their particularization to them along with these names being fit for their condition, deficiency, and weakness. If the particularization and affixation were removed, these designations would be (i.e. their meaning) in accordance with the names (of Allah); however, the congruence of these words does not necessitate congruency of their true reality and those actually named.[49]

In layman's terms the words used to describe Allah that coincide with words used to describe the creation only have a similarity as relates to the words and what they generally imply; however, the specific reality

---

48. Al-Qawaa'id Al-Mithla.

49. Fiqh-ul-Asma Al-Husna.

is totally different and that which is specific to the creation is nowhere near equal and comparable to Allah. Thus the striking of a similitude, the drawing a likeness, the comparing and contrasting, all are impossible for humans to do as relates to Allah due to the words and or names being comprehended as relates to what they imply generally but uncomprehended as relates to Allah's specific reality.

ALLAH (الله); the third word within the basmalah referred to as the expression of majesty indicates a characteristic attributed to the Lord of the universe.

Ibn Mundah said:

> So His name Allah is knowledge as it relates to Him. He prevents anyone among His creation from naming themselves with it, or a deity besides Him being invoked with it. He made it the starting point to faith (i.e. the first shahadah), a post/pillar of Islam, and a word of truth and sincerity. Moreover; (He made it) conflicting with its opposite (in meaning and what it entails) and with -there being- association (as results to what it means and entails) with it insomuch that the one who utters it -i.e. on the battlefield, etc- is withheld from being killed. Furthermore; It is used to commence obligatory acts, to conclude oaths, to seek refuge from the Shaitan, and to initiate and conclude varying things. Thus His name is blessed and there is no deity in truth other than Him.[50]

Sheikh Muhammad ibn Salih Al-Uthaymin said: "The expression of majesty is knowledge as pertains to the Originator (of all things). It is a name that all other names are pursuant."[51]

The magnificence of this name is appreciated when understanding what it entails. The scholars of Islam clearly illustrate what the name indicates, that being that He is the sole possessor of divinity. In other words, only He merits deification, servitude, and worship on account of Him being characterized with divinity, a trait not shared by anyone or thing within the creation. On account of this, all other names are pursuant to this name. They detail and elucidate His qualities of divinity

---

50. Kitab-ut-Tawheed.

51. Sharh Al-Usul As-Sittah.

that are unparalleled, perfect, and flawless.

The following is an abridged translation which emphasizes the aforementioned point. Some parts of the Sheikh's speech were omitted in order to spare the reader from recurring statements that may seem redundant. Sheikh Abdur Razzaq Al-Badr said:

> Indeed from what is very beneficial concerning the subject of the beautiful names is comprehension of its categories with regards to their meanings, as they are categorized, in that regard, into several categories:
>
> 1. Whatever indicates qualities related to His Being/Self. These qualities, which the Lord has not and will not cease to be described with, are neither separate from His Being/Self, nor connected to His Will. From these names are the following:
>
>   - Al-Hayy: It indicates the immutable quality of life.
>   - Al-Aleem: It indicates the immutable quality of knowledge.
>   - As-Samee: It indicates the immutable quality of hearing.
>   - Al-Baseer: It indicates the immutable quality of sight.
>   - Al-Qawi: It indicates the immutable quality of strength.
>   - Al-Ali: It indicates the immutable quality of uloo (the state of being high/exalted above everything)
>   - Al-Aziz: It indicates the immutable quality of might.
>   - Al-Qadeer: It indicates the immutable quality of ability/ omnipotence.
>
>   All of these qualities are related to His Being, due to them being innate to His Essence i.e., neither being separate from it nor connected to His Will.
>
> 2. Whatever indicates qualities related to action. These qualities are directly connected to His volition, if He wills He does it and if He wills He does not do it. From these names are the following:
>
>   - Al-Khaliq: It indicates the immutable quality of creating.
>   - Ar-Razzaq: It indicates the immutable quality of giving provision.
>   - At-Tawwab: It indicates the immutable quality of accepting repentance.
>   - Al-Ghafoor: It indicates the immutable quality of forgiveness.
>   - Ar-Raheem: It indicates the immutable quality of acting mercifully.

- Al-Muhsin: It indicates the immutable quality of acting proficiently.

- Al-Afwu: It indicates the immutable quality of pardoning.

All of these qualities are related to action on account of being connected to the volition (of Allah).

3. Names that indicate infallibility, reverence, and absolving the Lord -glorified and exalted is He- from deficiencies and impairments. Also from whatever is not befitting of His majesty, perfection, and grandiose nature. For instance His names like Al-Quddus, As-Salaam, and As-Subbuh all refer to infallibility, reverence, and absolving the Lord from whatever is not befitting for Him. Likewise they indicate this flawless nature being free of defects and blemishes, or that there is for Him a partner, counterpart, and equal among His creation. Therefore, He is considered to be exalted above whatsoever negates qualities of perfection, majesty, and grandeur.

4. Names that indicate various qualities in an all encompassing sense and not simply one meaning. Certainly from His names are those which indicate an abundance of qualities, and a name of this nature comprises all of them along with such a name being that which (as a result of these other perfect attributes) indicates one -main- quality. Among these names are Al-Majeed, Al-Hameed, Al-Atheem, As-Samad, and As-Sayyid....Al-Hameed is He Who possesses all that is commendable, that being every perfect quality, thus every quality from His qualities are praiseworthy. Al-Atheem is He Who possesses complete grandeur/sublimity as pertains to His names, attributes, and actions. He is described with a multitude of qualities of perfection, majesty, and beauty.[52]

In concluding this point; the categories mentioned previously give us a better understanding of why Allah is the greatest name among the Lord of the universe's names. As they detail the perfect, sublime, and supreme qualities and actions of Allah that expound -in overtly unambiguous terms- on His quality of divinity along with precise clarification as to why He alone merits servitude and worship. They also illustrate the grave error of he who would deify other than Allah, especially while knowing what the name Allah means and entails, and what it makes necessary upon every human being to enact.

---

52. Fiqh-ul-Asma Al-Husna.

AR-RAHMAN (الرحمن) AND AR-RAHEEM (الرحيم): these are the fifth and sixth words within the phrase and are the second and third names of Allah found therein. They are names that point to the attribute of mercy, as a result Allah is described with such. Logically, the question may arise, is there a difference between these two names? This is a subject which the scholars of Islam hold differences of opinion, and they are as follows:

- There is no difference in meaning, but emphasis as relates to the attribute of mercy being factually affirmed for Allah.
- Ar-Rahman is a word in the exaggerative tense which indicates vast and extensive mercy which encompasses all of creation i.e. Muslim and Non-Muslim, whereas Ar-Raheem is a specified mercy that is particular to the believers.
- Ar-Rahman is a description of Allah, whereas Ar-Raheem indicates the gesture of acting mercifully.

Although the majority of scholars held the second opinion, the third statement—and Allah knows best—appears to be the correct opinion. Sheikh Abdur Razzaq Al-Badr states:

> Certainly these two names are reported in many places coupled within the Quran. Both of them indicate the immutable quality of mercy for Allah, nonetheless the coupling of these two names signifies this description and the acquiring of its impact and its effect on those whom it is connected to. Hence Ar-Rahman is He Who mercy is His description, while Ar-Raheem is He Who acts mercifully with His servants. On account of this He -the Exalted- says: **'And He acted mercifully (raheem) with the believers'; 'He is, with them, kind and acts mercifully (Raheem)'** [At-Taubah: 117].
>
> It was not reported as -rahman with His servants- or -rahman with the believers-, on the contrary Ar-Rahman comes on the scale of *fa'lan* which points to a perfect and essential established quality i.e. amid His attributes is mercy, whereas Ar-Raheem points to the extending of it to its receiver i.e. the one He acts with mercifully.[53]

In light of the aforementioned benefits concerning the words within the *Basmalah* and their meanings, it becomes explicitly clear that

---

53. Fiqh-ul-Asma Al-Husna.

the translation "In the name of Allah The Most Merciful and Most Compassionate" and whatever is similar to it, do not illustrate in totality the profound and outstanding meaning of this phrase. Although it gives us a rudimentary understanding, it falls short as relates to all aspects of the phrase. A better translation would be "Seeking assistance and reward with all the names of Allah, the Most Merciful and The One Who acts mercifully I write (or whatever action on behalf of which the *Basmalah* is pronounced)" and Allah knows best.

THE IMPORTANCE OF PRONOUNCING THE BASMALAH

The commencement of one's writings with the *Basmalah* is a matter expressly encouraged by the people of knowledge due to it being an emulation of Allah's book, as it commences with the *Basmalah*, likewise each chapter (except At-Taubah) begins with the *Basmalah*. In addition, it is an emulation of the Prophet ﷺ as he commenced his letters with it. This is displayed in an authentic narration collected by Imam Al-Bukhari—i.e. hadith 7—wherein a letter was sent to Heraclius from the Messenger -sallahu alayhi wa sallam- which he read to a group of Quraish after questioning them about the Prophet and his message. The following is the text of the letter as found in the narration:

Bis-mil-llah-ir-Rahman-ir-Raheem

From Muhammad Allah's servant and messenger

To Heraclius the emperor of Rome

Peace be upon those that follow guidance. As for what follows; Indeed I invite you with the invitation of Islam, submit yourself (i.e. to Allah willfully) and be safe, on account of that Allah will give you your reward two-fold; however, if you turn away then upon you is (not only your sin) the sin of your subjects.

"O People of the Book!" Come to a common word between us and you, that being that we will not worship anyone except Allah, and will not associate partners with Him. Additionally none among us will take others as lords besides Allah. If they turn away thereafter, then say: bear witness that we surrender to Allah wilfully." [*Ali-Imraan: 64*]

Thus this is from the guidance of Allah's Messenger ﷺ and there is neither guidance that is better than his, nor a better example than him to be followed.

WHAT IS THE DIFFERENCE BETWEEN THE BASMALAH AND THE TASMIYYAH?

The difference between the *Basmalah* and the *Tasmiyyah* is one of great importance, especially when attending circles of knowledge in which fiqh jurisprudence is the subject, on account of the fact that when each is mentioned two distinct things are implied. The *Tasmiyyah* is the statement "*Bis-mil-llah*" without the addition of Allah's two names Ar-Rahman and Ar-Raheem. If "*Bis-mil-llah*" is accompanied with those two names it is deemed to be the *Basmalah* and not the *Tasmiyyah*. Hence, the intent of "pronounce the *Tasmiyyah* prior to performing ablution" is say "*Bis-mil-llah*" only. Or if one said "Don't eat until you say the *Tasmiyyah*" what he means is don't eat unless "*Bis-mil-llah*" is said.

Some of the people of knowledge held the opinion that the *Tasmiyyah* was every phrase in which the expression of majesty is uttered. This opinion implies that the *Basmalah* is the *Tasmiyyah* due to Allah's name being uttered; however, every *Tasmiyyah* is not the *Basmalah*, due to the *Basmalah* being a particular expression wherein the expression of majesty is mentioned, it being "*Bis-mil-llah-ir-Rahman-ir-Raheem.*" This position suggests that the *Basmalah* is a more particularized expression, whereas the *Tasmiyyah* is more general and encompasses all phrases that mention Allah's name, and Allah knows best.

Among the most remarkable of wonders and the greatest of signs indicating the ability of the Triumphant King are six principles that Allah elucidated with a blatantly obvious clarification for the general masses, being far above the suspicions of the naysayers/skeptics.

This statement of the author alludes to the fact that Allah—glorified and exalted is He—has detailed that which the creation requires, in order to be successful in the next life. This point is illustrated throughout the text of the Quran and in the authentic Sunnah of His Messenger. Allah says:

وَنَزَّلْنَا عَلَيْكَ ٱلْكِتَبَ تِبْيَنَا لِكُلِّ شَيْءٍ وَهُدًى وَرَحْمَةً وَبُشْرَىٰ لِلْمُسْلِمِينَ

And We sent down the Book making clear all things. A guidance, mercy, and glad tidings for those who submit wilfully (i.e. to Allah). [An-Nahl: 89]

The scholars of Quranic Exegesis—past and present—elucidate the intent of "making clear all things" stating that it is all of that which is required of belief, statement, and action; that leads to success and a state of well being in the next life. The following are some of their statements.

Al-Baghawi said: "A clarification 'all things' i.e. that he needs from commands and prohibitions, lawful and unlawful, prescribed punishments and rulings."[54]

At-Tabaraani said about the portion "Making clear all things": "From the affairs of the religion."[55]

Ibn Jarir At-Tabari said: "He sent down to you—O Muhammad—this Quran clarifying all of what the people need as pertains to knowledge of

---

54. Mu'aalim At-Tanzeel.

55. At-Tafseer Al-Kabeer.

the lawful and unlawful, and rewards and punishments."[56]

Sheikh Abdur Rahman ibn Nasir said:

(Making clear all things) i.e. as pertains to the fundamentals of the religion and its subsidiary issues, its rulings concerning the two abodes, and everything the servant needs; indeed it is a delineator as pertains to that and it is most precise by way of distinct verbal expressions and obvious meanings.[57]

More verses illustrating this point are as follows:

الٓر كِتَٰبٌ أُحۡكِمَتۡ ءَايَٰتُهُۥ ثُمَّ فُصِّلَتۡ مِن لَّدُنۡ حَكِيمٍ خَبِيرٍ

Alif Lam Ra. A Book the verses therein are perfect then explained in detail by One All-Wise and Well Acquainted (i.e. Allah). [Hud: 1]

مَّا فَرَّطۡنَا فِى ٱلۡكِتَٰبِ مِن شَىۡءٍ

...We have not neglected anything in the Book... [Al-An'am: 38]

وَكَذَٰلِكَ نُفَصِّلُ ٱلۡأَيَٰتِ وَلِتَسۡتَبِينَ سَبِيلُ ٱلۡمُجۡرِمِينَ

And like that do We explain the verses in detail so that the way of the criminals may be manifest. [Al-An'am: 55]

وَكُلَّ شَىۡءٍ فَصَّلۡنَٰهُ تَفۡصِيلًا

...And We have explained everything in detail with a full explanation. [Al-Israa: 12]

مَا كَانَ حَدِيثًا يُفۡتَرَىٰ وَلَٰكِن تَصۡدِيقَ ٱلَّذِى بَيۡنَ يَدَيۡهِ وَتَفۡصِيلَ كُلِّ شَىۡءٍ وَهُدًى وَرَحۡمَةً لِّقَوۡمٍ يُؤۡمِنُونَ

...It (the Quran) is not fabricated speech, but a confirmation of that which was before it, a detailed explanation of everything, a guidance, and a mercy

---

56. جامع البيان في تفسير القرآن.

57. Tayseer Al-Karim Al-Rahman.

for a people who believe. [Yusuf: 111]

وَمَا كَانَ هَٰذَا ٱلۡقُرۡءَانُ أَن يُفۡتَرَىٰ مِن دُونِ ٱللَّهِ وَلَٰكِن تَصۡدِيقَ ٱلَّذِى بَيۡنَ
يَدَيۡهِ وَتَفۡصِيلَ ٱلۡكِتَٰبِ لَا رَيۡبَ فِيهِ مِن رَّبِّ ٱلۡعَٰلَمِينَ

And this Quran is not that which was invented by anyone other than Allah; on the contrary, it is a confirmation for that which was before it, and a detailed explanation of the Book in which there is no doubt is from the Lord of all that exists. [Yunus: 37]

Not only is this sentiment repeated within the authentic Sunnah, but is stated in the simplest of manners. The following narration is collected by At-Tabaraani and is declared to be authentic by Sheikh Al-Albani, and is narrated on the authority of Abu Dharr. He said:

Allah's Messenger ﷺ left us and there wasn't a bird flapping its wings in the air except that he mentioned to us, on account of it, knowledge. He ﷺ said: 'Nothing remains that brings you closer to paradise and distances you further from the fire except that I have mentioned it to you.'[58]

This reality was not only witnessed by the noble companions, but also by those who had interactions with the Muslims during that time. Imam Muslim has, within his authentic collection, a narration on the authority of Salman Al-Farisi were he stated:

The idol worshippers said to us: 'Indeed your companion -i.e. The Prophet- teaches you everything, even the etiquettes for relieving oneself.' I replied: 'Of course, he forbade each of us from cleaning himself with his right hand or facing the qibla, likewise he forbade using dung and bones (for cleaning purposes), and that each of us should use no less than three pebbles for cleansing.'[59]

Therefore everything within this worldly life from belief, statement,

---

58. Al-Mu'jam Al-Kabir: 1647.

59. Muslim: 262.

and action which draws the servant close to Allah, and to His mercy and forgiveness; despite what the affair may be, it is made explicitly clear within Allah's perfect legislation insomuch that the most ignorant of people comprehend it. Thus all praise is due to Allah He Who has illuminated the path of success and true prosperity to His servants and has made the paths that contradict and oppose this equally clear in order for the intelligent to avoid.

Thereafter—i.e. this clarification—many among the intellectuals of this world and the erudite thinkers among the descendants of Adam erred with regards to them except a small number among a minority.

Author

Extracted from this portion of the author's statement is a beneficial point, supported and derived from the text of the Quran and Sunnah. This point being that misguidance, its paths, and its people are plentiful and far outnumber the truth. The following are some Quranic verses that indicate the plethora of misguided paths and teachings.

Commentator

اللَّهُ وَلِيُّ ٱلَّذِينَ ءَامَنُوا۟ يُخْرِجُهُم مِّنَ ٱلظُّلُمَٰتِ إِلَى ٱلنُّورِ

Allah is the Wali of those who believe, He extracts them from (various forms of) darkness into the light... [Al-Baqara: 257]

هُوَ ٱلَّذِى يُنَزِّلُ عَلَىٰ عَبْدِهِۦ ءَايَٰتٍۭ بَيِّنَٰتٍ لِّيُخْرِجَكُم مِّنَ ٱلظُّلُمَٰتِ إِلَى ٱلنُّورِ

It is He Who sends down to His servant clear verses in order to extract you out of darknesses bringing you into light... [Al-Hadid: 9]

$$\text{رَسُولًا يَتْلُوا عَلَيْكُمْ ءَايَنتِ اللَّهِ مُبَيِّنَتٍ لِّيُخْرِجَ الَّذِينَ ءَامَنُوا وَعَمِلُوا الصَّلِحَتِ مِنَ الظُّلُمَتِ إِلَى النُّورِ}$$

A messenger reciting to you Allah's clear verses in order to extract those who believe and do righteous deeds from darknesses into light... [At-Talaq: 11]

Ibn Kathir said:

> The Exalted informs us that He guides to the paths of tranquility whoever conforms to His pleasure (i.e. conforms to the guidance that -by way of it- achieves Allah's pleasure). Hence He removes His believing servants from the darknesses of disbelief, doubt, and suspicion placing them in clear, apparent, obvious, and illuminated truth, -til he eventually said- The Exalted made singular the verbal expression of light, but used the plural for darknesses because the truth is one; however, disbelief has many types and all are false.

Narrated on the authority of Abdullah ibn Masud who said:

> *Allah's Messenger* ﷺ *drew for us a straight line and then said 'This is Allah's path.' Thereafter he drew lines to the right and left of it and said 'These are diverging paths and upon each of them there is a devil inviting towards it. Then he recited the verse 'And this is My straight path so follow it and do not follow other paths that will divert you from My path...'*[60]

When this point is properly understood, a person logically understands that the truth is one and its people are a minority among mankind. This is a point oft-repeated throughout the Quran and Sunnah. Hence the majority should never be used as a yardstick to determine what is correct.

If you were to obey whomever is on the earth they would mislead you from Allah's path... [Al-An'am: 116]

---

60. Musnad Imam Ahmad.

إِنَّهُ ٱلْحَقُّ مِن رَّبِّكَ وَلَٰكِنَّ أَكْثَرَ ٱلنَّاسِ لَا يُؤْمِنُونَ

...Certainly it is the truth from your Lord; however, most of mankind do not believe. [Hud: 17]

وَمَا أَكْثَرُ ٱلنَّاسِ وَلَوْ حَرَصْتَ بِمُؤْمِنِينَ

And most of mankind will not believe, although you earnestly desire it. [Yusuf: 103]

الٓمٓرۚ تِلْكَ ءَايَٰتُ ٱلْكِتَٰبِۗ وَٱلَّذِىٓ أُنزِلَ إِلَيْكَ مِن رَّبِّكَ ٱلْحَقُّ وَلَٰكِنَّ أَكْثَرَ ٱلنَّاسِ لَا يُؤْمِنُونَ

Alif-Lam-Mem-Raa; these are the verses of the Book. That which was revealed to you from your Lord is the truth; however, most of mankind do not believe. [Ar-Ra'd: 1]

The Quranic verses that illustrate this reality are plentiful. Likewise there is a narration collected by Imam Al-Bukhari within his authentic collection, on the authority of Abdullah ibn Masud, therein he stated:

We were in a tent along with the Prophet ﷺ and he said, 'Would you all be pleased to be a fourth of the people of paradise?' We replied, 'Yes.' He said, 'Would you all be pleased to be a third of the people of paradise?' We said, 'Yes.' He -then- said, 'Would you all be pleased to be half of the people of paradise?' We responded, 'Yes.' Thereafter he said, 'I swear by Him in Whose Hand is Muhammad's soul, undoubtedly I hope you all will be half of the people of paradise, as none will enter paradise except a believing soul. And you all, in comparison to the polytheists, are nothing except like a white hair on a black ox, or a black hair on a red ox.[61]

Narrated on the authority of Abu Huraira; the Prophet ﷺ said:

Islam began as something strange and will return just as it began as something strange, thus glad tidings of good are for the strangers.[62]

---

61. Bukhari: 6528.

62. Muslim: 145.

Imam An-Nawawi said, while expounding on the intent of the narration:

> Al-Qadhi (i.e. Iyyadh) said, 'The apparent meaning of the narration is general, it being that Islam began with a handful of people and or minority, then it spread and became visible. Eventually deficiency and impairment will follow it to the point that nothing will remain except as pertains to a handful of people and or minority.'

Ibn Qayyim Al-Jawziyya said:

> These individuals are the commended and envied strangers. On account of them being scarce among the people they are dubbed strangers, and the majority of people are upon other than this characteristic. Consequently the adherents to Islam among the people are strangers. The believers among the adherents of Islam are strangers. The people of knowledge among the believers are strangers. The adherents to the Sunnah, those who distinguish it from desires and innovation are strangers. The caller to the Sunnah being patient with the harms of those who oppose, they are the most severe in terms of strangeness; however, they are Allah's people in reality. There is no strangeness upon them (in reality), on the contrary their strangeness is only amid the majority.[63]

This reality of scarceness as relates to the people of truth outside and in Islam is a reality acknowledged by people of knowledge and understanding with regards to Allah's perfect legislation. It is a reality that necessitates our caution as relates to the adopting of beliefs and practices that are solely contingent upon what is seen from the majority. On the contrary these matters should be enacted after a clear basis is found within the text prior to enactment. Unfortunately this cautionary approach in these later times is viewed as odd and peculiar resulting in the person exhibiting such caution being viewed by many as strange or unusual. We ask Allah for safety and security during these clear times of confusion.

---

63. Madaarij-us-Salikin.

The First Principle

Author

Ikhlas as relates to deen for Allah's sake alone without any—attributing of a—partner with him. Likewise a clarification of its opposite which is—deemed or dubbed—Shirk with Allah. In addition, the majority of the Quran, as relates to this fundamental, is a clarification from varying perspectives with utilization of speech that the most unintelligent of people comprehend.

Then there transpired, as pertains to the majority of the Islamic Nation, what transpired, as the Shaitan presented Ikhlas to them in the image of prejudice towards the righteous, and dereliction of their rights. Whereas Shirk with Allah, he presented it to them in the image of love for the righteous and emulation of them.

Commentator

The author's statement is similar to his statement within the introduction; however, this statement is more particularized. The introduction presents the contrast between the early generation of Muslims and their understanding as relates to Islam, and later generations with regards to how their practice conflicts with these early generations, but this presentation is in an all inclusive and unrestricted sense thus encompassing all matters in the religion. However, this first principle highlights the contrast in understanding as pertains to the matter of Ikhlas specifically, and that which nullifies it i.e. Shirk. Thus the following matters are of great importance to the reader:

- What is Ikhlas?
- What is intended by Deen?
- What is Shirk?

WHAT IS IKHLAS?

Ikhlas is the purification and refinement of the heart by purging it of all blemishes of Shirk. This definition, although worded differently by the scholars, ultimately is its intent. The following are some scholars' speech concerning its meaning:

Sheikh Abdullah Al-Qaraawi said: "Ikhlas is an action of the heart and it is loving Allah and desiring His Face."[32] Sheikh Hafidh ibn Ahmad Al-Hakami stated: "Ikhlas is purification of actions from all blemishes of Shirk by way of a sound intent."[33] Sheikh Muhammad ibn Salih Al Uthaymin said:

> Ikhlas is refinement, and the intent of this is that a man desires by way of his acts of worship Allah's face and achieving His paradise insomuch that he does not worship along with Him other than Him, neither a close angel nor a sent prophet.[34]

Ibrahim ibn-ush-Sheikh Salih Al-Kuraisi said:

> Ikhlas linguistically means purification, and legislatively (i.e. in Islam) it is loving Allah, desiring His Face, and purification of worship making all of it exclusively for Him alone from all aspects of Shirk.[35]

Based on the aforementioned Islamic technical definitions to Ikhlas, it is of the utmost importance for the reader to understand three affairs directly connected to it, in order to better comprehend it.

FIRST: Ikhlas is an action of the heart, thus being unseen to man and impossible for man to determine if it actually is present with others

---

32. As-Sharh Al-Muyassir, pg 201.

33. Ma'aarij-ul-Qubul.

34. Sharh Thalatha-til-Usool.

35. Tanbihaat Al-Mukhtasirah.

or not. No one or nothing is able to determine this aspect of the heart except Allah. The following authentic narration elucidates this point:

> *Usamah ibn Zayd said: Allah's Messenger ﷺ sent us to Huraqah a tribe of Juhainah. So we launched an offense against them during the early hours of the morning and defeated them. (During that moment) I and a man from the Ansar followed an individual among them and when we eventually surrounded him he said, 'There is no deity in truth except Allah' on account of that the Ansari refrained from further advancement against him; however I struck him with my spear until he died. When we returned (to Medinah) the incident reached the Prophet ﷺ so he said to me, 'O Usamah! Did you kill him after he said there is no deity in truth except Allah?' He replied, 'O Messenger of Allah! He was only seeking protection (i.e. by uttering those words).' So he repeated, 'Did you kill him after he said there is no deity in truth except Allah?' He did not cease repeating it to me until I wished that I had not accepted Islam before that day.*[36]

Within another chain of transmission found with Imam Muslim, the Prophet ﷺ at one point said to Usamah, "Did you not rip open his heart to determine if it professed it or not?!" Imam An-Nawawi said, while expounding on this statement,

> Did you not rip open his heart in order to analyze if the heart uttered and believed it and if it was actually within it or was not within it but merely something uttered upon the tongue?! In other words, you are unable to do this so restrict yourself to the tongue (i.e. what he uttered) and do not request other than that.[37]

This understanding was exemplified within the statement of the second khalifah, Umar ibn-ul-Khattab when he said:

> *People were taken to account based on revelation during the time of Allah's Messenger ﷺ but now revelation is cut, so now we hold you to account based on the apparent of your actions. So whoever manifests good deeds we will trust and be close to him and there is nothing upon us as relates to what he conceals, as Allah will take him to account for that. And whoever displays evil, we do not trust nor believe*

---

37. Sharh Sahih Muslim.

him, even if he said that his intent is good."[38]

SECOND: Although Ikhlas is a portion of the intent, it is not the intent in its entirety. This point is very important to comprehend especially when analyzing statements of Allah and His Messenger ﷺ wherein intent is used. Accurate comprehension of this affair assists the person in proper contextualization of Allah and His Messenger's ﷺ speech. The following statement of the Prophet ﷺ is presented in order to illustrate this point:

> *Actions are only by way of intent, and for every man there is only what he intends. Thus whoever's migration is towards Allah and His Messenger, then his migration is towards Allah and His Messenger. Likewise whoever's migration is for obtaining an aspect of worldly life, or in order to marry a woman, then his migration is for whatever he migrated towards.* [39]

Before proceeding, it becomes imperative to understand the phrase "Actions are only by way of intent" due to actions being confined to the intention, thus what is intended here? The scholars held two widespread understandings to this statement. The first is; actions, their acceptance and validity, are based on intent. The second is; the cause of actions is their intent, in other words the intent is the cause behind the implementation of the action. So what is the proper interpretation here?

The former minister of Islamic Affairs for the Kingdom of Saudi Arabia, Sheikh Salih Alish-Sheikh states:

> The first opinion is correct because affirmation of the incentive behind actions—stemming from action of the heart—is not the intent of the narration, and this is apparent from its context. On the contrary, what is solely intended is the stipulation of intent for an action as the intent is the validator of the action. This is clear because the Prophet ﷺ said, 'Actions are only by way of intent, and for every man there is only what he intends' a clarification of what the Islamic Legislation demands of him, not on account of what is present as pertains to occurrence. On

---

38. Bukhari: 2641.

39. Bukhari: 1.

account of this we say that the more acceptable interpretation to his ﷺ statement 'Actions are only by way of intent' is actions are only valid and accept or invalid on account of the intent, and for every man, reward and compensation stemming from his actions are only based on what he intends."[40]

This illustrates the reality that Ikhlas is not synonymous with intent, on the contrary it is a component of the intent, but not the intent in its entirety. Thus we're left with the question, what are all the components that make the intent?

Sheikh Salih Alish-Sheikh clarifies this point:

The intent has two components. The intent affixed to the act of worship and the intent affixed to the deity. As for the intent affixed to the act of worship it is that which the scholars of Islamic Jurisprudence apply when they present prerequisites (i.e. to acts of worship). The first prerequisite (to acts of worship) is the intent. They intend by that; the intent directed towards the act of worship and it is the distinction between varying acts of worship. Distinguishment of the prayer from fasting, distinguishment of the obligatory prayer from the voluntary i.e. the heart distinguishes what he implements of one act of worship from another. For example, a man comes to the masjid wanting to pray two units of prayer, his heart distinguishes these two units. Is it tahiyyat-ul-masjid or two unit sunnahs? Or is it two units for Istikhaarah? Thus the heart distinguishes one act of worship from another, this is the intent referred to by the scholars of jurisprudence found within the books of Islamic Jurisprudence and it is the intent directed towards the act of worship.

The second component; The intent directed towards the deity, this is what is spoken about by—usage of—the phrase Ikhlas. Purifying the heart, cleansing the intent, refining the action making it solely for Allah. This is frequently applied by verbal expressions such as intent, Ikhlas, and want/desire."[41]

THIRD: Ikhlas—normally translated as sincerity—is obligatory upon every Muslim, and is a prerequisite for the acceptance of worship. This fact is illustrated throughout the text of the Quran and Sunnah and is

---

40. Sharh Arba'een An-Nawawiyyah.

41. Sharh Arba'een An-Nawawiyyah.

found in both by way of straightforward commands that necessitate obligation.

$$وَمَا أُمِرُوا إِلَّا لِيَعْبُدُوا اللَّهَ مُخْلِصِينَ لَهُ الدِّينَ حُنَفَاءَ$$

And they were not commanded except but to worship Allah being strictly sincere and monotheistic to Him...
[Al-Bayyinah: 5]

$$إِنَّ الْمُنَافِقِينَ فِي الدَّرْكِ الْأَسْفَلِ مِنَ النَّارِ وَلَن تَجِدَ لَهُمْ نَصِيرًا ﴿١٤٥﴾ إِلَّا الَّذِينَ تَابُوا وَأَصْلَحُوا وَاعْتَصَمُوا بِاللَّهِ وَأَخْلَصُوا دِينَهُمْ لِلَّهِ فَأُولَٰئِكَ مَعَ الْمُؤْمِنِينَ ۖ وَسَوْفَ يُؤْتِ اللَّهُ الْمُؤْمِنِينَ أَجْرًا عَظِيمًا ﴿١٤٦﴾$$

Undoubtedly the hypocrites are in the lowest depths of the fire and you will never find a helper for them. Except those—among them—that repent, rectify (their wrong), adhere to Allah, and purify their religious practice making it solely/sincerely for Allah, they are those who will be with the believers and Allah will give the believers a tremendous reward. [An-Nisaa: 145-146]

$$إِنَّا أَنزَلْنَا إِلَيْكَ الْكِتَابَ بِالْحَقِّ فَاعْبُدِ اللَّهَ مُخْلِصًا لَهُ الدِّينَ ﴿٢﴾ أَلَا لِلَّهِ الدِّينُ الْخَالِصُ$$

Indeed We sent down to you the Book in truth so worship Allah being sincere to Him in religious practice. Is not the religion solely for Allah sincerely? [Az-Zumar:2-3]

Furthermore we have a narration authentically traced back to Abu Hurairah where he quotes the Prophet ﷺ saying the following:

Certainly Allah does not look at neither your outward appearance nor wealth, on the contrary He looks at your hearts and actions.[42]

---

42. Muslim: 2564.

In addition, there is the powerful narration authentically traced to An-Nu'man ibn Basheer where he quotes the following from Allah's Messenger ﷺ:

> Certainly, there is within the body a piece of flesh, if it is rectified the entire body is rectified, and if it is corrupt the entire body is corrupt. Yes certainly, it is the heart."[43]

Ibn Rajab Al Hanbali comments on the aforementioned narration, he said:

> It alludes to the rectification of the servant's physical movements via body limbs, his avoidance of prohibited acts, and his caution from dubious matters being contingent upon the rectification of his heart's actions. If his heart is sound; by having nothing within it except love for Allah, love of whatsoever Allah loves, along with fear of Allah, and fear of falling into whatever Allah hates; then the movements of his body limbs are rectified. Thus what stems from this is the avoidance of prohibited acts and protection from dubious matters as a precaution from falling into the forbidden. In contrast to if the heart is corrupt as conformity to the desires a demand of what it loves overwhelms him, although Allah hates it. Consequently all physical movement of the body becomes corrupt as it emanates sinful and dubious behavior according to the hearts conformity to lust.[44]

We ask Allah for success in purifying our hearts, correcting our intent, and actualizing ikhlas in order for our acts of worship to be accepted.

WHAT IS INTENDED BY DEEN?

Deen is an Arabic word often translated into English as religion. Although the word religion gives us a general understanding of the term deen, analyzation of its intent from the Islamic perspective is still essential. Moreover, it's important to highlight the definition of the word religion, it is a personal set or institutionalized system of religious attitudes, beliefs, and practices.

---

43. Al-Bukhari: 52 and Muslim: 1599.

44. Jaami-ul-Uloom wal-Hikm.

As for the meaning of Deen Sheikh Muhammad ibn Salih Al Uthaymin put forth a brief summary of the word. He stated:

> Deen its intent is action on account of the phrase (deen) having two distinctions. Deen as relates to action, and deen as relates to recompense. Thus the Exalted's statement: **'The Owner/Possessor of the day of Deen'** what is meant is reward/recompense. Whereas His statement: **'..and He is pleased with Islam as your Deen'** what is intended here is action.[45]

Therefore Deen is a word that encompasses all of that which the servant devotes to Allah of worship (from statements and actions of the heart, tongue, and body limb) and this worship is what He commanded them to execute, and Allah knows best.

WHAT IS SHIRK?

Shirk, an Arabic word, is normally translated as polytheism i.e. the belief and practice of worship to multiple deities. However, in Islamic context the word is more concise than that. Shirk is to make an aspect of the creation equal to the Creator i.e. Allah as relates to characteristics specific to Him. This pertains to His exclusive qualities of lordship, divinity, and with regards to His names and attributes. In addition, included within the meaning of Shirk is to attribute aspects of these qualities to other than Him. And this is what is meant when we find statements or actions deemed to be Shirk within the text.

Sheikh Abdur Rahman ibn Hasan Alish-Sheikh said, while detailing the magnitude of Shirk:

> On account of that it is obligatory for the servant to be extremely fearful from committing Shirk, due to it being the most repugnant of abominable deeds, and the most oppressive of wrongs. Likewise it is a diminishing of the Lord of all existence, it's a diverting of His exclusive rights to other than Him, and it is equalizing other than Him with Him.[46]

---

45. Sharh Al-Arba'een An-Nawawiyyah.

46. Fath-ul-Majeed.

Sheikh Ibrahim ibn-ush-Sheikh Salih Al-Khuraisi said: "Shirk is an equalization of something other than Allah with Allah in that which is a particularized characteristic of Allah."[47] Sheikh Salih Al-Fawzan said: "Shirk is to direct any act of worship to other than Allah."[48]

The difference in wording of the scholars regarding the definition to Shirk does not negate the congruence of their meanings. With respect to the subject of Shirk, it is essential for the reader to grasp some important affairs related to it, and they are as follows:

FIRST: Shirk has two distinct categories; major and minor Shirk, and the previously mentioned definition encompasses both types. Thus both types of Shirk are from the gravest of sins; however, major Shirk is of a greater magnitude of sin than minor due to it being disbelief, whereas minor Shirk is not disbelief. The Prophet صَلَّىٰاللَّهُعَلَيْهِوَسَلَّمَ said, in an authentic narration from Anas ibn Malik, the following:

The gravest of major sins are Shirk with Allah, killing a person, disobedience to parents, and false speech or false testimony.[49]

Sheikh Zayd Al Madkhali, while commenting on the narration, said: "And the most tremendous of major sins is Shirk with Allah regardless if it is major or minor; however, Major Shirk is more grave and dangerous, and it is to direct an aspect of worship to other than Allah."[50]

Sheikh Bin Baz was asked: Are the means to Shirk graver (in sin) than the gravest of major sins? He replied:

Yes. Innovation and the means to Shirk are graver than the classification of major sins. The levels are: Major Shirk, then minor, subsequent to that is innovation, then the major sins, and thereafter the minor sins.[51]

---

47. At-Tanbihaat Al-Mukhtasira.

48 . Duroos fi Sharh Nawaaqid Al-Islam.

49. Collected by Al-Bukhari and Muslim.

50. Awn-ul-Ahad As-Samad Sharh Adab Al Mufrad.

51. From the website of the Sheikh under the section—فتاوى الدروس-.

SECOND: The scholars detail important differences between Major and Minor Shirk in order for it to be understood properly and the reality of both to be reflected upon and avoided. The differences are as follows:

- Major Shirk expels one from Islam, whereas Minor does not.
- Major Shirk nullifies all good deeds, whereas Minor nullifies the action with which it is associated.
- Major Shirk confines its doer to the Hell Fire forever, whereas Minor Shirk does not.
- Major Shirk will not be forgiven if its doer dies without repentance, whereas Minor Shirk the scholars differ concerning it. Among them some say it is not forgiven, while others say the doer is under the will of Allah i.e. if He Wills He shall forgive him or if He Wills He shall punish him.

THIRD: Minor Shirk, like Major, has two distinct classifications. The first being apparent and or visible aspects, and this relates to actions of the body limbs, and verbal utterances and or expressions. The second being hidden and or inward, and this relates to actions of the heart. The following examples are presented in order to simplify these classifications and their differences.

WEARING AMULETS, TALISMANS, AND OR LUCKY CHARMS

This is the wearing or hanging of an object, regardless of what its material may be, as a means to ward off evil or adversity. Sheikh Salih Al Fawzan said,

> At-Tamimah (translated as amulets, talismans, lucky charms, etc) are beads hung on children to protect them from the evil eye. Likewise whatever resembles it from that which is hung (i.e. on the neck) regardless if it's beads or other than that (material).[52]

---

52. I'aanat-ul-Mustafeed.

Uqbah ibn Aamir Al-Juhani said:

A group of people approached Allah's Messenger ﷺ nine of them he concluded pledges with; however, he refrained from one among them. So they said, 'O Messenger of Allah! You concluded pledges with nine among them yet you abandon this one?' He ﷺ replied, 'On him is a lucky charm.' So he took his hand and then cut it and thereafter concluded the pledge with him. He ﷺ said, 'Whoever wears a tamimah has undoubtedly committed Shirk'.[53]

This type falls under the classification of apparent/visible acts related to body limbs.

SWEARING BY OTHER THAN ALLAH

Swearing by someone other than Allah, with well known verbal expressions that denote a solemn declaration or affirmation is Shirk due to the statement being a form of exalting the one sworn by. Sheikh Salih Al Fawzan said, "Swearing is an oath, and it emphasizes a decision by mentioning a revered figure from the aspect of specification. Reverence/Exaltation is a right due to Allah the Exalted, thus it is not permissible to swear by anyone other than Him."[54] The Sheikh also said, "Swearing is exaltation—by the tongue—of the one sworn by."[55]

Qutailah—a woman from Juhaina—said:

A Jew came to the Prophet ﷺ and said, 'Indeed you all make rivals with Allah and worship others besides Him. You all say "What Allah and you will" and you say, "I swear by the Kabah."' Consequently the Prophet ﷺ ordered them by saying, 'Whoever desires to swear should say "by the Lord of the Kabah", and he should say "what Allah wills and thereafter what you will."'

---

53. Al-Musnad of Ahmad.

54. Aqidat-ut-Tawheed.

55. I'aanat-ul-Mustafeed.

This type falls under the classification of apparent/visible acts related to verbal utterances or expressions.

SHOWING OFF (RIYAA)

Showing off is to perform an act of worship with a divided intent. Although the performer of the act wants to please Allah and obtain His reward, he also desires the pleasure of someone else for a worldly benefit, even if it is as simple as praise from the people. Sheikh Hafidh ibn Ahmad Al-Hakami said, "If the motive for the action is desiring Allah and the abode of happiness in the next life; however, showing off infiltrates it as pertains to beautification and amelioration of it, then that is what the Prophet referred to as Minor Shirk and explained it as Riyaa (i.e. showing off)."

Abu Saeed Al Khudri said:

Allah's Messenger ﷺ came upon us while we were speaking about Al-Masih Ad-Dajjal, so he said, 'Shall I not inform you about what I fear for you more than Al-Masih Ad-Dajjal?' We replied with yes, so he said, 'The Hidden Shirk. A man stands to pray and as a result he beautifies his prayer for whomever sees among man.'[56]

This type falls under the classification of hidden/inward acts related to the heart.

FOURTH: Minor Shirk is a means to Major Shirk.

Undoubtedly Minor Shirk is a direct means to Major Shirk. This reality is evident when examining aspects of Minor Shirk and how the difference between it and its counterpart from Major Shirk are simple differences easily comprehended. For instance; wearing lucky charms is Minor Shirk from one perspective and Major Shirk from another, with a slight difference between the two. Sheikh Salih Al Fawzan said,

If he believes that lucky charms are a means to remove adversity or repel it, this is Minor Shirk due to Allah not prescribing it as a means. As for if he believes it repels or removes adversity in and of itself, this is

---

56. Ibn Majah: 4204.

Major Shirk on account of being reliant on other than Allah. [57]

Another example: swearing by others besides Allah is Minor Shirk from one perspective and Major Shirk from another. Sheikh Muhammad Al Wasaabi said, "Swearing by other than Allah is considered to be Minor Shirk; however, if exaltation for whoever is being sworn by from the creation is situated within the heart that resembles exaltation of Allah, it is Major Shirk."[58] To elaborate, the mere utterance of swearing by someone other than Allah is a verbal exaltation of the one being sworn by; however, this exaltation is not found within the heart. It's an expression denoting exaltation and the importance of a thing. For this reason only important things or people are sworn by, something that is frequently seen in western society e.g. "I swear by my unborn child" or "That's on my mother" or "I swear by my dead grandmother" etc. Thus the mere expression is Minor Shirk, in contrast to one having exaltation for that thing in his heart as well as the verbal utterance that denotes exaltation. Undoubtedly this is Major Shirk.

I ask Allah for protection from all forms of Shirk.

In addition, the majority of the Quran, as relates to this fundamental, is a clarification from varying perspectives with utilization of speech that the most unintelligent of people comprehend.

Author

The entire Quran is replete in clarifying the affair of worship to Allah alone, and it presents it from varying perspectives. Imam ibn Qayyim Al Jawziyya said,

> The majority of the chapters of the Quran, on the contrary all of the chapters of the Quran are inclusive of the two types of tawheed.

Commentator

---

57. Aqidat-ut-Tawheed.

58. Mukhtasir Sabil Al-Huda war Rashaad.

Rather, we say a complete statement that every verse within the Quran is inclusive of tawheed, an evidence for it, and a caller towards it. Thus the Quran—at times—it is a notification about Allah; His names, attributes, and actions; this is the knowledge related informational aspect of tawheed. Or it calls towards His worship alone without any partners along with forgoing all of what is worshiped besides Him, and this is the intention and request related tawheed. As for commands, prohibitions, obliging with obedience to Him; these are the rights of tawheed and what completes it. Furthermore it's a notification about His generosity towards the adherents of tawheed and His obedience, also how He interacted with them in this worldly life and how He will honor them in the next life; this is the rewards of tawheed. Likewise it is a notification about the idolaters and how He acted with them in this worldly life from exemplary punishment and what He will cause to happen to them in the end from torment; this is the recompense for whoever exits from the rulings of tawheed.[59]

Author

Then there transpired, as pertains to the majority of the Islamic Nation, what transpired, as the Shaitan presented Ikhlas to them in the image of prejudice towards the righteous, and dereliction of their rights. Whereas Shirk with Allah, he presented it to them in the image of love for the righteous and emulation of them.

Commentator

Shaitan is a term, in the Islamic technical sense, applied in a general manner to every aspect of creation that is insolent, rebellious, and disobedient. As relates to jinn and men it is specific to those that rebel against Allah's commands, perseveres in disobedience to Him, and goes throughout the land causing corruption and mischief. When applied with the definite article (i.e. the) it refers to the creature among the race of jinn called Iblis, the chief deceiver who strives to lead the descendants of Adam astray.

Al-Imam Abul Faraj ibn-ul-Jawzi said:

When the human being was created, composed within him were lust

---

59. Madaarij As-Saalikin.

and desires in order to obtain—by way of their utilization—whatsoever benefits him. Likewise placed within him was anger in order to repel—by way of its utilization—whatsoever harms him. He was given intellect like a discipliner that orders him with justice as pertains to what he acquires (of benefit) and avoids (of harm), whereas the Shaitan was created as an instigator towards excessiveness (i.e. exceeding set limits) in what he (i.e. man) acquires and avoids. Thus it is incumbent upon the intelligent person to be cautious of this enemy who manifested his hostility during the era of Adam, and has sacrificed his age and self in corrupting the well being of the progeny of Adam. [60]

Allah mentions within the Quran the events that took place after Adam's creation as a lesson for man to reflect, and understand the goal of the Shaitan as relates to man's destruction. The following verses elucidate these events:

وَإِذْ قَالَ رَبُّكَ لِلْمَلَٰٓئِكَةِ إِنِّى جَاعِلٌ فِى ٱلْأَرْضِ خَلِيفَةً ۖ قَالُوٓا۟ أَتَجْعَلُ فِيهَا مَن يُفْسِدُ فِيهَا وَيَسْفِكُ ٱلدِّمَآءَ وَنَحْنُ نُسَبِّحُ بِحَمْدِكَ وَنُقَدِّسُ لَكَ ۖ قَالَ إِنِّىٓ أَعْلَمُ مَا لَا تَعْلَمُونَ ۝ وَعَلَّمَ ءَادَمَ ٱلْأَسْمَآءَ كُلَّهَا ثُمَّ عَرَضَهُمْ عَلَى ٱلْمَلَٰٓئِكَةِ فَقَالَ أَنۢبِـُٔونِى بِأَسْمَآءِ هَٰٓؤُلَآءِ إِن كُنتُمْ صَٰدِقِينَ ۝ قَالُوا۟ سُبْحَٰنَكَ لَا عِلْمَ لَنَآ إِلَّا مَا عَلَّمْتَنَآ ۖ إِنَّكَ أَنتَ ٱلْعَلِيمُ ٱلْحَكِيمُ ۝ قَالَ يَٰٓـَٔادَمُ أَنۢبِئْهُم بِأَسْمَآئِهِمْ ۖ فَلَمَّآ أَنۢبَأَهُم بِأَسْمَآئِهِمْ قَالَ أَلَمْ أَقُل لَّكُمْ إِنِّىٓ أَعْلَمُ غَيْبَ ٱلسَّمَٰوَٰتِ وَٱلْأَرْضِ وَأَعْلَمُ مَا تُبْدُونَ وَمَا كُنتُمْ تَكْتُمُونَ ۝ وَإِذْ قُلْنَا لِلْمَلَٰٓئِكَةِ ٱسْجُدُوا۟ لِـَٔادَمَ فَسَجَدُوٓا۟ إِلَّآ إِبْلِيسَ أَبَىٰ وَٱسْتَكْبَرَ وَكَانَ مِنَ ٱلْكَٰفِرِينَ ۝ وَقُلْنَا يَٰٓـَٔادَمُ ٱسْكُنْ أَنتَ وَزَوْجُكَ ٱلْجَنَّةَ وَكُلَا مِنْهَا رَغَدًا حَيْثُ شِئْتُمَا وَلَا تَقْرَبَا هَٰذِهِ ٱلشَّجَرَةَ فَتَكُونَا مِنَ ٱلظَّٰلِمِينَ ۝ فَأَزَلَّهُمَا ٱلشَّيْطَٰنُ عَنْهَا فَأَخْرَجَهُمَا مِمَّا كَانَا فِيهِ ۖ وَقُلْنَا ٱهْبِطُوا۟ بَعْضُكُمْ

---

60. Talbis Iblis, pg. 45.

61

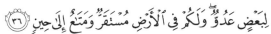

لِبَعْضٍ عَدُوٌّ وَلَكُمْ فِي ٱلْأَرْضِ مُسْتَقَرٌّ وَمَتَٰعٌ إِلَىٰ حِينٍ ﴿٣٦﴾

And when your Lord said to the Angels, 'Surely I will place on the earth successors (i.e. of man one generation succeeding another).' They said, 'Will you place (in it) those who will cause corruption and shed blood while we glorify your praises and sanctify you?' He said, 'I am All Knower of whatsoever you do not know.' And He taught Adam the names of all things, then displayed them to the angels and said, 'Inform me about the names of these things if you are truthful!' The Angels replied, 'Glory be to You, we have no knowledge except that which You taught us, certainly You are the All-Knowing and All-Wise.' He said, 'O Adam! Inform them of their names' so when he informed them of their names Allah said, 'Did I not tell you that surely I am more knowledgeable concerning the unseen of the heavens and earth, and more knowledgeable as pertains to what you reveal and conceal?' And when We said to the Angels, 'Prostrate yourselves to Adam!' They prostrated except Iblis, he refused and was arrogant, thus being among the disobedient to Allah. And We said 'O Adam! You and your wife dwell within paradise and eat freely in comfort, but do not come near this tree lest you be among the oppressive.' Then the Shaitan caused them to slip from it (paradise), so they were expelled from their former situation. We said, 'Drop from here as some of you are enemies of each other, on earth will be a place of settlement and enjoyment for a time.' [Al-Baqara: 30-36]

وَإِذْ قَالَ رَبُّكَ لِلْمَلَٰٓئِكَةِ إِنِّي خَٰلِقٌۢ بَشَرًا مِّن صَلْصَٰلٍ مِّنْ حَمَإٍ مَّسْنُونٍ ﴿٢٨﴾ فَإِذَا سَوَّيْتُهُۥ وَنَفَخْتُ فِيهِ مِن رُّوحِي فَقَعُوا۟ لَهُۥ سَٰجِدِينَ ﴿٢٩﴾ فَسَجَدَ ٱلْمَلَٰٓئِكَةُ كُلُّهُمْ أَجْمَعُونَ ﴿٣٠﴾ إِلَّآ إِبْلِيسَ أَبَىٰٓ أَن يَكُونَ مَعَ ٱلسَّٰجِدِينَ ﴿٣١﴾ قَالَ يَٰٓإِبْلِيسُ مَا لَكَ أَلَّا تَكُونَ مَعَ ٱلسَّٰجِدِينَ ﴿٣٢﴾ قَالَ لَمْ أَكُن لِّأَسْجُدَ لِبَشَرٍ خَلَقْتَهُۥ مِن صَلْصَٰلٍ مِّنْ حَمَإٍ مَّسْنُونٍ

قَالَ فَٱخْرُجْ مِنْهَا فَإِنَّكَ رَجِيمٌ ﴿٣٤﴾ وَإِنَّ عَلَيْكَ ٱللَّعْنَةَ إِلَىٰ ﴿٣٣﴾
يَوْمِ ٱلدِّينِ ﴿٣٥﴾ قَالَ رَبِّ فَأَنظِرْنِىٓ إِلَىٰ يَوْمِ يُبْعَثُونَ ﴿٣٦﴾ قَالَ فَإِنَّكَ مِنَ
ٱلْمُنظَرِينَ ﴿٣٧﴾ إِلَىٰ يَوْمِ ٱلْوَقْتِ ٱلْمَعْلُومِ ﴿٣٨﴾ قَالَ رَبِّ بِمَآ أَغْوَيْتَنِى
لَأُزَيِّنَنَّ لَهُمْ فِى ٱلْأَرْضِ وَلَأُغْوِيَنَّهُمْ أَجْمَعِينَ ﴿٣٩﴾ إِلَّا عِبَادَكَ
مِنْهُمُ ٱلْمُخْلَصِينَ ﴿٤٠﴾ قَالَ هَٰذَا صِرَٰطٌ عَلَىَّ مُسْتَقِيمٌ ﴿٤١﴾ إِنَّ
عِبَادِى لَيْسَ لَكَ عَلَيْهِمْ سُلْطَٰنٌ إِلَّا مَنِ ٱتَّبَعَكَ مِنَ ٱلْغَاوِينَ ﴿٤٢﴾

And when your Lord said to the Angels, 'Surely I will create a human (Adam) from dried clay of variable sludge. So when I shape him and blow into him my (created) soul, then prostrate to him.' Thus every Angel prostrated to him. Except for Iblis, he refused to be among those that prostrated. Allah said, 'O Iblis! What is with you, that you do not be among the prostrators?!' He said, 'I am not one that prostrates to a human while you created him from dried clay of variable sludge.' He—Allah—said, 'Then leave from here undoubtedly you are casted out. Likewise the curse will be upon you til the day of recompense.' He—Iblis—said, 'O my Lord, give me respite til the day they are resurrected.' Allah said, 'Certainly you are among those reprieved, until the day of the appointed time.' Iblis said, 'My Lord because you misled me, I will beautify for them (children of Adam) error within the earth, and will mislead them all, except your chosen servants. Allah said, 'This is the path that will lead straight to Me. Undoubtedly you will have no authority over My servants except with those who follow you from the Ghaween (those that know the truth but abandon it deliberately).' [Al-Hijr: 28-42]

Thus the Shaitan embarked upon the goal of misleading the descendants of Adam by usage of deception and trickery. He pledged to beautify the pathways of falsehood and error in order to achieve his goal. Al-Imam Abul Faraj ibn-al-Jawzi simplifies the methods used by the Shaitan in an attempt to mislead the progeny of Adam, he said:

Talbis (normally translated as deceit) is packaging falsehood in the image of truth, and ghuroor (normally translated as delusion i.e. a false opinion) is a type of ignorance that makes binding a corrupt belief to be valid and the repugnant to be good. Its cause is the presence of a doubt that makes this incumbent, as Iblis enters upon man in accordance with his ability, and his ability increases or decreases to the extent of their vigilance and or heedlessness, additionally, to the extent of their ignorance and or knowledge.

So understand that the heart is like a fortress upon which there are walls. These walls have doors that have gaps within them. The inhabitant of this fortress is the intellect and Angels frequently visit the fortress. On the side of the fortress is its outer perimeter that has therein the inclinations. The devils frequently come and go to the outer perimeter without obstruction, and the war between the inhabitants of the fortress and those on the outer perimeter is ongoing. The devils do not cease to circle the fortress seeking heedlessness from its guards and penetration of its gaps (the weak points). Therefore it is incumbent for the guard to be well acquainted with all of the fortress' doors that he has been entrusted to defend and all of its weak points. He should never become laxed in guarding it not for one moment, as the enemy surely is never laxed. [61]

In light of the aforementioned, concerning the Shaitan and his role with the progeny of Adam, the final and obvious conclusion drawn is that the Shaitan is a clear and overt enemy as Allah describes him within His noble book:

يَٰٓأَيُّهَا ٱلنَّاسُ كُلُوا۟ مِمَّا فِى ٱلْأَرْضِ حَلَٰلًا طَيِّبًا وَلَا تَتَّبِعُوا۟ خُطُوَٰتِ ٱلشَّيْطَٰنِ ۚ إِنَّهُۥ لَكُمْ عَدُوٌّ مُّبِينٌ ﴿١٦٨﴾ إِنَّمَا يَأْمُرُكُم بِٱلسُّوٓءِ وَٱلْفَحْشَآءِ وَأَن تَقُولُوا۟ عَلَى ٱللَّهِ مَا لَا تَعْلَمُونَ ﴿١٦٩﴾

O mankind! Eat from the lawful and pure things within the earth and do not follow the steps of the Shaitan, certainly he is a clear enemy. He only orders you to commit evil deeds, immorality, and to say about Allah what you do not know. [Al-Baqara: 168-169]

---

61. Talbis Iblis, pg 64.

Al-Imam Ibn Kathir said: "Your enemy the Shaitan only orders you with evil actions, and the most distasteful of them is fornication/adultery, etc. More distasteful than that is speech about Allah without knowledge as the disbeliever and every innovator indulge in this."

The verse elucidates the two perspectives utilized by the Shaitan to mislead the descendants of Adam, that being the enticing towards one's lust, cravings, and desires; and the other being the presenting of doubts and gaslighting in order to confuse the servant concerning Allah and His straight path. Both of these perspectives are included within the term "trials of life" from which we seek refuge with Allah.

Abu Huraira said:

> Allah's Messenger ﷺ would supplicate with 'O Allah I seek refuge with you from the torment of the grave, the punishment of the fire, the trials of life and death, and from the trial of Al-Masih Ad-Dajjal.' [62]

Sheikh Abdullah Ali-Basaam said:

> The Prophet ﷺ would supplicate with this, he instructed the usage of it, and made the place for this supplication at the end of the prayer on account of it being the position of response. It is comprised of seeking refuge from the torment of the grave, the punishment of the fire, the cravings of the worldly life and doubts therein, the misleading of the Shaitan at the time of death, the trials of the grave that which is the means of his torment, and the trials of the dajjals; those that display themselves to the people in the image of truth while they are actually camouflaging falsehood. The greatest of them, as pertains to trial (upon the people) is he who is authentically reported to appear during the last days, and we seek refuge with Allah from trials/tribulation. [63]

The Sheikh, while explaining the trials of life, entered within its meaning the doubts hurled into the hearts of men that are presented in order to cause confusion as relates to the truth. These doubts are more severe than the perspective of lusts and desires, as the verse illustrates and lists in simplistic terms that which was least in terms of evil, to that which was

---

62. Al-Bukhari: 1377 and Muslim: 588.

63. Tayseer Al-Alaam Sharh Umdatil Ahkam.

greater. Speaking about Allah without knowledge was the gravest of evils mentioned on account of evil emanating from it (e.g. Allah is the third of three, Allah is everywhere, Allah is a spirit, etc), and this occurs by way of confusion held in the heart for Allah and His guidance. Confusion that manifested on account of doubts presented by the Shaitan.

In this regard Allah gives us many examples from nations within the past that were destroyed on account of their corrupt understanding that sprung forth due to the deception of the Shaitan and his doubts. Among these examples are the people of Nuh. Allah says about them:

$$\text{قَالَ نُوحٌ رَّبِّ إِنَّهُمْ عَصَوْنِي وَٱتَّبَعُوا۟ مَن لَّمْ يَزِدْهُ مَالُهُۥ وَوَلَدُهُۥٓ إِلَّا خَسَارًا ۝ وَمَكَرُوا۟ مَكْرًا كُبَّارًا ۝ وَقَالُوا۟ لَا تَذَرُنَّ ءَالِهَتَكُمْ وَلَا تَذَرُنَّ وَدًّا وَلَا سُوَاعًا وَلَا يَغُوثَ وَيَعُوقَ وَنَسْرًا ۝}$$

Nuh (Noah) said: 'My Lord! Indeed they disobey me and follow him whose wealth and children give him no increase except in loss. In addition they plotted a major plot by saying: 'You will not abandon your gods, nor will you abandon Wadd, Suwa, Yaghuth, Yauq, nor Nasr.' [Nuh: 21-23]

Imam Ash-Shawkani said:

> Muhammad ibn Kab said, 'These are names of righteous people that existed between the time of Adam and Nuh. Thereafter a people emerged emulating them in worship, so Iblis said to them, 'If you make images of them it will invigorate and incite you towards worship." Consequently they did this, thereafter a people emerged and Iblis said to them, "Those that came before you worshiped them so you should worship them." Thus the commencement of worshiping idols was at that point in time, and these images were given these names due to them being in the image of those people.'[64]

We ask Allah to increase us in beneficial knowledge, that it be a protection which repels such doubts.

---

64. Fath-ul-Qadeer.

The Second Principle

Author

Allah commands unity as pertains to religion and prohibits division therein. Hence He clarified this by way of a categorical explanation that the common folk comprehend. Likewise, He prohibited us from being like those—prior to us—who split and differed, consequently being destroyed. He adds clarity to this by what is reported, from the most remarkable of things,—found—within the sunnah. Thereafter, division within the fundamentals of the religion and its subsidiary issues became knowledge and comprehension of the religion, whereas unity in the religion became that which no one spoke about except a heretic or one mentally challenged.

Commentator

The command for unity and the Muslim nation being unified is a directive that is clear, overt, and obvious; likewise the prohibition from division, differing, splitting, and disunity has an explicit mention within the text of the Quran and Sunnah. Among the most well known of verses illustrating this command and prohibition is verse 103 in Ali-Imran. Allah says what is translated to mean:

وَٱعْتَصِمُواْ بِحَبْلِ ٱللَّهِ جَمِيعًا وَلَا تَفَرَّقُواْ وَٱذْكُرُواْ نِعْمَتَ ٱللَّهِ عَلَيْكُمْ إِذْ كُنتُمْ أَعْدَآءً فَأَلَّفَ بَيْنَ قُلُوبِكُمْ فَأَصْبَحْتُم بِنِعْمَتِهِۦ إِخْوَٰنًا وَكُنتُمْ عَلَىٰ شَفَا حُفْرَةٍ مِّنَ ٱلنَّارِ فَأَنقَذَكُم مِّنْهَا ۗ كَذَٰلِكَ يُبَيِّنُ ٱللَّهُ لَكُمْ ءَايَٰتِهِۦ لَعَلَّكُمْ تَهْتَدُونَ

And cling to the Rope of Allah altogether, and do not be divided. Remember Allah's favor upon you, as you were enemies and He joined your hearts together resulting in you all becoming brothers by His favor. You all were on the brink of a pit of fire and He saved you from it. Like that Allah makes explicitly clear His verses in order for you to be guided.

Imam Ash-Shawkani said: "He the glorified instructed them with unity with regards to adherence to the religion of Islam or to the Quran, and prohibited them from division that emanates from differing in (matters of) the religion."[65]

Sheikh Salih Al-Fawzan said:

The Arab, prior to the advent of the Prophet ﷺ, were divided amongst themselves and frequently fought one another establishing long wars among themselves e.g. the war of Dahis and Ghabraa (named after two horses. This battle lasted for 40 years), the Day of Buath (the final battle between the Aus and the Khazraj before the Prophet's migration to Yathrib), and wars that were prolonged between them lasting for 100 years or longer. They were in a constant state of conflict among themselves harboring hostility and hatred along with raids and incursions until Allah bestowed His favor upon them by sending the Prophet ﷺ.

The Prophet ﷺ invited them to the worship of Allah alone without partners, likewise to unity and brotherhood among themselves. So whoever answered his call, Allah wrote for them prosperity/wellbeing, and they gathered under the banner of monotheism, and under the leadership of the Prophet ﷺ resulting in the termination of what was between them of enmity. Consequently they became brothers loving one another after they had been enemies separating from one another.[66]

Other verses that illustrate the command for unity and the prohibition from division are as follows:

---

65. Fath-ul-Qadeer.

66. الاجتماع و نبذ الفرقة.

وَأَنَّ هَٰذَا صِرَٰطِي مُسْتَقِيمًا فَٱتَّبِعُوهُ ۖ وَلَا تَتَّبِعُوا۟ ٱلسُّبُلَ فَتَفَرَّقَ بِكُمْ عَن سَبِيلِهِۦ ۚ ذَٰلِكُمْ وَصَّىٰكُم بِهِۦ لَعَلَّكُمْ تَتَّقُونَ

Undoubtedly this is My Straight Path so follow it and do not follow other paths that consequently separate you from His Path, this He has ordained in order for you to become pious. [Al-An'am: 153]

إِنَّ ٱلَّذِينَ فَرَّقُوا۟ دِينَهُمْ وَكَانُوا۟ شِيَعًا لَّسْتَ مِنْهُمْ فِى شَىْءٍ ۚ إِنَّمَا أَمْرُهُمْ إِلَى ٱللَّهِ ثُمَّ يُنَبِّئُهُم بِمَا كَانُوا۟ يَفْعَلُونَ

Indeed those who divide their religion and separate into sects, you have nothing to do with them. Their affair is with Allah, subsequently He will announce to them what they used to do. [Al-An'am: 159]

شَرَعَ لَكُم مِّنَ ٱلدِّينِ مَا وَصَّىٰ بِهِۦ نُوحًا وَٱلَّذِىٓ أَوْحَيْنَآ إِلَيْكَ وَمَا وَصَّيْنَا بِهِۦٓ إِبْرَٰهِيمَ وَمُوسَىٰ وَعِيسَىٰٓ ۖ أَنْ أَقِيمُوا۟ ٱلدِّينَ وَلَا تَتَفَرَّقُوا۟ فِيهِ ۚ كَبُرَ عَلَى ٱلْمُشْرِكِينَ مَا تَدْعُوهُمْ إِلَيْهِ ۚ ٱللَّهُ يَجْتَبِىٓ إِلَيْهِ مَن يَشَآءُ وَيَهْدِىٓ إِلَيْهِ مَن يُنِيبُ

He (Allah) has legislated for you that which He ordained for Noah and that which We revealed to you (i.e. Muhammad), and that which We ordained for Abraham, Moses, and Jesus—proclaiming—establish the religion and do not be divided therein... [Ash-Shura: 13]

وَأَطِيعُوا۟ ٱللَّهَ وَرَسُولَهُۥ وَلَا تَنَٰزَعُوا۟ فَتَفْشَلُوا۟ وَتَذْهَبَ رِيحُكُمْ ۖ وَٱصْبِرُوٓا۟ ۚ إِنَّ ٱللَّهَ مَعَ ٱلصَّٰبِرِينَ

And obey Allah and His Messenger, and do not be at variance with one another lest you become emasculated and your strength departs... [Al-Anfal: 46]

These verses indicate the fundamental ruling concerning differing and separation in matters of religion, that being prohibition. Consequently differing in this regard is considered to be blameworthy and evil, and the removal of unity is indicative of Allah's removal of mercy upon the people. Allah says:

$$وَلَوْ شَآءَ رَبُّكَ لَجَعَلَ ٱلنَّاسَ أُمَّةً وَٰحِدَةً وَلَا يَزَالُونَ مُخْتَلِفِينَ ۝ إِلَّا مَن رَّحِمَ رَبُّكَ وَلِذَٰلِكَ خَلَقَهُمْ وَتَمَّتْ كَلِمَةُ رَبِّكَ لَأَمْلَأَنَّ جَهَنَّمَ مِنَ ٱلْجِنَّةِ وَٱلنَّاسِ أَجْمَعِينَ ۝$$

And if your Lord willed, surely He could have made them one nation, but they will not cease to differ. Except those whom your Lord bestows mercy and on account of that He created them... [Hud: 118-119]

The outstanding scholar of hadith of recent time, Sheikh Muhammad ibn Nuh Nasruddin Al-Albani said—concerning the verse-: "If those to whom which Allah acts mercifully do not differ, and the only people that differ are the people of falsehood, then how can it be perceived that differing is a mercy?!"[67]

DIFFERING AND ITS VARYING TYPES

Although the fundamental ruling concerning differing in the religion is prohibition, it is incumbent to comprehend that every type of differing is not the same. Despite differing being fundamentally prohibited, this is as relates to differing deemed to be clashing with revelation; however, some differing is encouraged, and other differing may take the ruling of allowance. Nonetheless these types of differing are not referred to in the aforementioned verses.

Sheikh Muhammad Al-Imam—one of the leading scholars of hadith in Yemen today—said concerning this matter:

> The distinction (i.e. between these types) is very important to comprehend and adhere to. The sects in which the adherents to the Sunnah, past and present, pass judgment against as pertains to

---

[67] Sifat Salat-in-Nabi.

innovation and partisanship, is a blameworthy differing on account of these sects' contradiction towards a foundational aspect from the fundamentals (Usool) of the Adherents to the Sunnah or even more (than just one fundamental). Hence these sects are not attributable to the Sunnah except by abandonment of what they remove of it (i.e. from themselves by rejection of it).[68]

Thus differing is classified as having three distinct types and they are as follows:

- Differing as relates to diversification or variation.
- Differing as relates to comprehension.
- Differing as relates to contrast or opposition.

A detailed examination of all these types is important in order to fully comprehend what it is that Allah prohibits in His Noble Book.

DIFFERING AS RELATES TO DIVERSIFICATION AND OR VARIATION

Sheikh Muhammad Al-Imam stated concerning this type of difference, "This is from the legislation." In other words, this form of differing is actually legislated within the text. It pertains to the performance of acts of worship in more than one way. Every variation of how the act of worship is performed is legislated within the text, thus every person who performs the act regardless of what variation it may be is rewarded. The following are examples that illustrate this point.

EXAMPLE 1. THE ADHAN (CALL TO PRAYER)

The performance of the adhan is executed in more than one way. The first example consists of nineteen verbal phrases and or expressions derived directly from the text. The companion Abu Mahdhoorah is reported to have said the following:

---

[68] Al-Qawl Al-Hasan.

O Allah's Messenger (صَلَّى ٱللَّهُ عَلَيْهِ وَسَلَّمَ)! Teach me the prophetic tradition of calling to prayer. So he wiped my forehead and said, 'You should say: "Allah is the greatest (Allahu akbar), Allah is the greatest, Allah is the greatest, Allah is the greatest"; while your voice is raised high. Thereafter you say: "I bear witness that there is no deity in truth except Allah (Ash-hadu an laa illaha illa'llah), I bear witness that there is no deity in truth except Allah, I bear witness that Muhammad is Allah's Messeger, I bear witness that Muhammad is Allah's Messenger"; doing so while your voice is lowered. Thereafter raise your voice and say: "I bear witness that there is no deity in truth except Allah, I bear witness that there is no deity in truth except Allah, I bear witness that Muhammad is Allah's Messenger, I bear witness that Muhammad is Allah's Messenger, come to the prayer, come to the prayer, come to success, come to success". If it is the dawn prayer then say: "Prayer is better than sleep, prayer is better than sleep. (Continue until the end with) Allah is the greatest, Allah is the greatest, there is no deity in truth except Allah."[69]

Although this narration mentions nineteen verbal phrases, there is another method consisting of fifteen verbal phrases which differ with the aforementioned manner in which the call to prayer is made. Despite the variation in how the adhan is executed, both are firmly established in the text. It is reported that Abdullah ibn Zayd ibn Abdi Rabbih said:

When Allah's Messenger صَلَّى ٱللَّهُ عَلَيْهِ وَسَلَّمَ ordered a bell to be struck in order to gather the people for the prayer, a man carrying a bell in his hand appeared to me while I was asleep. I said (to him): 'O servant of Allah! Will you sell the bell?' He replied: 'And what will you do with it?' So I said: 'Use it so we can announce the (time for) prayer.' So he responded: 'Shall I not inform you of something which is better than this?' So I said of course. He continued: 'Say "Allah is the greatest, Allah is the greatest, Allah is the greatest, Allah is the greatest. I bear witness that there is no deity in truth except Allah, I bear witness that there is no deity in truth except Allah. I bear witness that Muhammad is Allah's Messenger, I bear witness that Muhammad is Allah's Messenger. Come to the prayer, come to the prayer. Come to success, come to success, Allah is the greatest, Allah is the greatest. There's no deity in truth except Allah..."[70]

---

69. Collected by Abu Dawud: 500.

70. Collected by Abu Dawud: 499, ibn Majah: 706, and others.

Both have different amounts of verbal phrases; however, both are legislated consequently making the implementation of both permissible and necessitating reward for conducting whichever of the two modes firmly established within the text.

EXAMPLE 2. THE OPENING INVOCATION OF THE PRAYER

The prayer has several different and varying opening invocations that can be uttered, all consisting of totally different verbal expressions, yet all are correct as all are legislated within the text. Here are some examples:

> *O Allah! Distance me from my sins just as you have distanced the east from the west. O Allah! Cleansed me of my sins just as you cleanse a white garment of filth. O Allah! Wash away my sins with water, snow, and hail.* [71]

> *I turned my face to He who is the Originator of the heavens and the earth as a monotheist and I am not among the idolaters. Undoubtedly my prayer, ritual sacrifice, my life, and my death are for Allah alone, Lord of all that exist, and there is no partner with Him. That is what I've been commanded, and I am from those that submit wilfully. O Allah; you are the King, there is no deity in truth except You. You are my Lord and I am your servant, I have oppressed myself and acknowledge my sins, so forgive me for all of my sins, undoubtedly no one forgives sins except You. Guide me to the best of conduct, no one guides to the best of it except You. Remove from me the worst of it, no one removes the worst of it (from a person) except You. Here I am at your service, all good is in Your Hand and evil is not attributed to You. I am on account of You and I turn to You. You are blessed and exalted, I seek forgiveness from you and turn to You in repentance.* [72]

> *O Allah, far above all deficiencies and faults are You declared and praise is for You. Blessed is Your name, exalted is Your grand nature, and there is no deity in truth besides You.* [73]

---

71. Narrated by Abu Huraira and collected by Bukhari and Muslim.

72. Muslim: 771.

73. Abu Dawud: 775.

EXAMPLE 3. THE TASLEEM TO CONCLUDE THE PRAYER

The tasleem also has varied ways of being performed, all of which are firmly established within the text. These variations are as follows:

- Turning one's head to the right while saying *"As salaamu alaykum wa rahmatullah"* then to the left while saying *"As salaamu alaykum wa rahmatullah."*
- Turning one's head to the right while saying *"As salaamu alaykum wa rahmatullahi wa barakaatuhu"* then to the left while saying *"As salaamu alaykum wa rahmatullah."*
- Turning one's head to the right while saying *"As salaamu alaykum wa rahmatullah"* then to the left while saying *"As salaamu alaykum."*
- Turn one's head slightly to the right while saying *"As salaamu alaykum"* and stopping there.

These examples should suffice in illustrating this category of differing and its ruling, and with Allah is success.

DIFFERING AS RELATES TO COMPREHENSION

This form of differing is also considered to be permissible. All differing parties are rewarded; however, only one statement—in matters of this nature—can be correct. This differing arises in matters wherein ijtihaad is employed to arrive at a ruling.

The Reviver of the Sunnah in Yemen Sheikh Muqbil ibn Haadi Al-Waadi'ee said:

> There are many affairs in which some scholars among the senior, virtuous, and well versed scholars understand (i.e. a particular way) in contrast to others that understand it differently. This is considered to be differing as relates to comprehension similar to what occurred among the Companions.[74]

The form of differing that occurred among the Companions, in which the Sheikh referred, can be found within a narration collected by Al-Imam Al

---

74. https://muqbel.net/fatwa.php?fatwa_id=3950.

Bukhari (946 and 4119). Abdullah ibn Umar narrated the following:

> *The Prophet* ﷺ *said to us after returning from the battle of the Confederates: 'None of you should pray the afternoon prayer except at Bani Quraitha.' So the afternoon reached some of us while we were still on the road (headed towards Bani Quraitha). As a result some of them said: 'We will not pray until we have arrived at it.' Yet others said: 'On the contrary; we will pray as he didn't intend that (i.e. the delaying of the prayer out of its time).' Consequently this dispute was mentioned to the Prophet* ﷺ *and he didn't reprimand anyone from among them.*

Ibn Rajab Al-Hanbali—the virtuous specialist in Islamic knowledge—said concerning this narration:

> There is no indication within the narration that every mujtahid (one who exerts himself in order to arrive at the correct and proper ruling on a thing based on scholarly jurist principles and precepts) is correct. On the contrary, within it is signification that the mujtahid, regardless if he is correct or mistaken, is not censored on account of his ijtihaad. Rather, if he is correct then for him are two rewards, and if he is mistaken then his mistake is relieved and for him is one reward on account of his ijtihaad.[75]

Al-Imam An-Nawawi said:

> The mujtahid is not rebuked as relates to whatever he does on account of his ijtihaad when he exerts efforts therein. Furthermore this narration is used as proof that every mujtahid is correct; however, others say that it is not explicitly clear that both groups were correct, on the contrary, it proves the disregard of rebuking them and there is no difference of opinion with regards to refraining from rebuking the mujtahid if he errs while exerting efforts in ijtihaad, and Allah knows best.[76]

Although some scholars held the position that the narration proves that every mujtahid is correct, that derivation is far-fetched and actually opposes another sound narration. The reality is every mujtahid is rewarded; one gets two rewards on account of his ijtihaad and being correct while another receives one reward for his ijtihaad but is not rewarded a second time on account of being incorrect in his conclusion. Amru ibn-ul-

---

75. Fath-ul-Bari.

76. Sharh Sahih Muslim.

Aas narrated from Allah's Messenger ﷺ the following:

> Whenever a judge makes a ruling while exerting efforts (i.e. to arrive at the truth) and he gets it correct, then for him is two rewards. Likewise when he judges and exerts efforts but is incorrect, then for him is a reward.[77]

Al-Imam An-Nawawi said as pertains to this narration:

> The Muslims have consensus that this narration pertains to a scholarly judge that is qualified to pass rulings. So if he is correct for him there are two rewards, a reward for his ijtihaad and a reward for being correct. If he is incorrect, then for him is one reward for his ijtihaad.[78]

DIFFERING AS PERTAINS TO CONTRADICTION AND OR OPPOSITION

This form of differing is forbidden. It is to contradict and or oppose whatsoever is found within the text to which the Islamic nation has consensus, regardless if it is a matter of creed or a matter that is physically implemented. Sheikh Muqbil said, concerning this type: "It is opposition to the clear and authentic evidence without any support (i.e. from the text)."[79]

Sheikh Muhammad Al-Imam said while expounding on this type: "It is clashing with the text and examples of this are present with the varying sects that separate from (the path/creed/methodology of) Ahlus Sunnah."[80]

To illustrate this fact further, the following examples of varying sects and their ideologies will be presented in order to demonstrate their opposition with that which the Islamic nation has consensus on, from the first generation until now.

1: THE JAHMIYYAH

---

77. Muslim 1716.

78. Sharh Sahih Muslim.

79. https://muqbel.net/fatwa.php?fatwa_id=3950.

80. القول الحسن في معرفة الفتن.

76

Sheikh Salih Al-Fawzan said about this group:

> They are the followers of Jahm ibn Safwan the Samarkandian, it is also said that he is Termezian (i.e. from Termez). He was a carrier of false ideologies and varying types of disbelief, as he negated the names and attributes of Allah, he spoke in accordance with the idea of jabr that being that the servant is forced to commit their actions and they neither have choice (i.e. free will) nor ability, he held the belief of irjaa and it is to say that faith is strictly awareness within the heart even if the actions did not affirm what is within the heart. Likewise (it is so) even if the tongue doesn't utter what is in accordance with it, and even if he doesn't act (accordingly) as long as he knows that Allah is his Lord and Muhammad ﷺ is His Messenger, then he is a believer.[81]

Thus the Sheikh listed several ideas of the Jahmiyyah that clash with the understanding and consensus of the Muslims from the first generation and those that follow them till this very day. From them are:

- Denying all the names and attributes of Allah, despite Allah's statement:

$$وَلِلَّهِ ٱلْأَسْمَآءُ ٱلْحُسْنَىٰ فَٱدْعُوهُ بِهَا ۖ وَذَرُوا۟ ٱلَّذِينَ يُلْحِدُونَ فِىٓ أَسْمَٰٓئِهِۦ ۚ سَيُجْزَوْنَ مَا كَانُوا۟ يَعْمَلُونَ$$

And to Allah belongs the best of names so invoke Him with them, and abandon those that deviate as pertains to His names, as they will be requited for what they use to do. [Al-A'raf: 180]

- The servant being forced to do whatsoever he does i.e. he has no free will, everything he does is imposed upon him without his choice, although Allah says:

$$إِنَّ هَٰذِهِۦ تَذْكِرَةٌ ۖ فَمَن شَآءَ ٱتَّخَذَ إِلَىٰ رَبِّهِۦ سَبِيلًا$$

Undoubtedly this is an admonition, so whoever wills (i.e. chooses) let him take a path (leading) to his Lord. [Al-Muzzamil: 19]

---

81. شرح لمعة الاعتقاد.

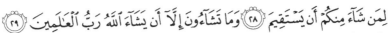

لِمَن شَآءَ مِنكُمْ أَن يَسْتَقِيمَ ۝ وَمَا تَشَآءُونَ إِلَّا أَن يَشَآءَ ٱللَّهُ رَبُّ ٱلْعَٰلَمِينَ ۝

To whomever among you that wills (i.e. desires/chooses) to be upright. And none of you wills (i.e. desires success in a matter by your actions) unless Allah, Lord of all existence wills (i.e. for you to be successful). [At-Takwir: 28-29]

- Faith being awareness of the heart alone, while excluding affirmation of what one is aware of. In addition they exclude statements of the tongue and actions of the body limb from faith, although Allah's Messenger ﷺ said:

Faith is 60 or 70 odd numbered branches. The most virtuous is the statement: 'There is no deity in truth except Allah' and the least of it is the removal of harm from the pathway, and shyness is a branch of faith.[82]

2: THE QADARIYYAH

They have two distinctive categories. The first of the two are the extreme of the Qadriyyah, i.e. negaters of the knowledge and writing of Allah who appeared during the latter part of the companions era. They are who the leading specialist among the Salaf declared to be disbelievers on account of their rejection of Allah's knowledge (i.e. of what would be prior to Him creating it by 50,000 years). [83]

Thus their deviation occurs in their creed as relates to aspects of Allah's predetermination. These aspects or affairs as relates to Allah's predetermination are vital and necessary in order for true belief in this regard to be actualized. So their clash with the text and consensus of the Muslims in this regard are as follows:

- Denial of Allah's infinite knowledge, and Him having full knowledge of His creation prior to it being created, despite Allah's statement:

ٱللَّهُ ٱلَّذِى خَلَقَ سَبْعَ سَمَٰوَٰتٍ وَمِنَ ٱلْأَرْضِ مِثْلَهُنَّ يَتَنَزَّلُ ٱلْأَمْرُ بَيْنَهُنَّ لِتَعْلَمُوٓا۟ أَنَّ ٱللَّهَ

---

82. Collected by Muslim.

83. موسوعة العقيدة والأديان والفرق والمذاهب المعاصرة.

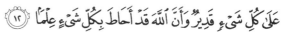

عَلَىٰ كُلِّ شَىْءٍ قَدِيرٌ وَأَنَّ ٱللَّهَ قَدْ أَحَاطَ بِكُلِّ شَىْءٍ عِلْمًا ۝

Allah is He Who created the seven heavens and the earth the like thereof. The command descends between them (i.e. the heavens and the earth) in order for you to know that Allah has power over all things, and that Allah encompasses all things as relates to knowledge (i.e. nothing is hidden from Him not even future occurrences). [At-Talaq: 12]

عَـٰلِمُ ٱلْغَيْبِ فَلَا يُظْهِرُ عَلَىٰ غَيْبِهِۦٓ أَحَدًا

All Knower of the unseen (this includes the unseen and unknown future) and He does not reveal to anyone His unseen. [Al-Jinn: 26]

• Denial of Allah's writing in the preserved tablet all that would occur within creation, despite Allah's statements:

أَلَمْ تَعْلَمْ أَنَّ ٱللَّهَ يَعْلَمُ مَا فِى ٱلسَّمَآءِ وَٱلْأَرْضِ ۖ إِنَّ ذَٰلِكَ فِى كِتَٰبٍ ۚ إِنَّ ذَٰلِكَ عَلَى ٱللَّهِ يَسِيرٌ

Do you not know that Allah is aware of what is in the sky and the earth? Undoubtedly it is in a book (written), and undoubtedly this is easy for Allah. [Al-Hajj: 70]

مَآ أَصَابَ مِن مُّصِيبَةٍ فِى ٱلْأَرْضِ وَلَا فِىٓ أَنفُسِكُمْ إِلَّا فِى كِتَٰبٍ مِّن قَبْلِ أَن نَّبْرَأَهَآ ۚ إِنَّ ذَٰلِكَ عَلَى ٱللَّهِ يَسِيرٌ

No calamity befalls within the earth nor upon yourselves except that it is (written) within a book prior to it coming into existence. Indeed that is easy for Allah. [Al-Haddid: 22]

Abdullah ibn Amru ibn Al-Aas conveyed the statement of Allah's Messenger ﷺ as follows:

Allah wrote the predetermination of all created beings prior to creating the heavens and the earth by 50,000 years and His throne was above the water.[84]

---

84. Collected by Muslim.

3: THE RAFIDAH (THE SHIITE)

Sheikh Muhammad ibn Salih Al-Uthaymin said concerning this group:

> They exceed limits as relates to the family of the Prophet ﷺ and declare to be a disbeliever or extremely sinful whomever opposed them from the companions. They have various groups, among them are the extremist that claim that Ali is a deity and others among them who are lesser in degree than that (as pertains to their fanaticism to Ali ibn Abi Talib). The first appearance of their innovation was during the reign of Ali ibn Abi Talib when Abdullah ibn Saba (A Jew who infiltrated the ranks of the Muslims to intentionally sow discord) said (i.e. to Ali) 'You are the deity.' Consequently Ali ordered them to be burned and their founder—Abdullah ibn Saba—fled to various cities.
>
> Their ideology as pertains to the attributes of Allah is multifarious. Among them is the one who makes a resemblance between Allah and His creation, then there is he who negates Allah's attributes, and others are on a middle course. They were dubbed Rafidah due to their rejection of Zayd ibn Ali ibn Husayn ibn Ali ibn Abi Talib after they asked him about Abu Bakr and Umar. He sought Allah's mercy for them thus they rejected him and distanced themselves from him. They dubbed themselves as Shiite on account of their claim that they sided with Ahlul Bayt, aided them, and sought restitution concerning their right to leadership. [85]

The Rafidah have many splinter groups among them with varying deviations e.g. The Zaidis, Alawis, Twelvers, Isma'iliyah, Houthis, etc. Although some sects among them have subsidiary issues that differ from others, their core belief with regards to Ali's succession and their hatred for Abu Bakr and Umar remain the same despite the following:

Abu Saeed Al-Khudri said:

There was something (i.e. of hostility) between Khalid ibn Al Walid and Abdur Rahman ibn Auf, as a result Khalid insulted him. Consequently Allah's Messenger ﷺ said, 'Do not revile any of my companions. Undoubtedly if any of you spent the like of mount Uhud in gold, you would not reach a dry bushel of any one of them nor half that.'[86]

---

85. شرح لمعة الاعتقاد.

86. Al-Bukhari and Muslim # 2541.

Abdur Rahman ibn Auf narrated the Prophet's ﷺ statement:

Abu Bakr is in Paradise, Umar is in Paradise, Uthman is in Paradise, Ali is in Paradise, Talha is in Paradise, Az-Zubayr is in Paradise, Abdur Rahman ibn Auf is in Paradise, S'ad ibn Abi Waqqas is in Paradise, Saeed ibn Zayd is in Paradise, and Abu Ubaydah ibn Al-Jarrah is in Paradise.[87]

Abdullah ibn Umar said:

We used to choose between the people during the time of the Prophet ﷺ concerning who is best. So we chose Abu Bakr, then Umar ibn Al-Khattab, then Uthman ibn Affan.[88]

These sects and their deviant ideas illustrate differing as pertains to contradiction and opposition to the text. It's this type of separation, conflict, opposition, and clashing with the source material that is intended in the authentic narration which describes the separation of the Muslim nation into 73 sects. The narration is as follows:

Muawiyya ibn Abi Sufyan said: "Allah's Messenger ﷺ stood among us one day and said, 'Indeed the people of the scripture before you separated into 72 sects upon desires. Alas this nation will separate into 73 sects upon desires, all shall be in the fire except one and it is the Jamaa'ah...'"[89]

Abul Ali Muhammad Al-Mubaarakfuri quotes Abu Mansoor Abdul Qahir ibn Tahir At-Tamimi's explanation of this narration, he said:

The authoritative writers of treatises know that He ﷺ did not intend that the blameworthy sects were separationist as relates to Islamic Jurisprudence with regards to the subject of permissible and forbidden. He ﷺ only intended, with rebuke, whomsoever opposed the adherents to the truth in the fundamentals of monotheism (Tawheed), the predetermination of good and evil, the provisions of

---

87. Tirmidhi # 3747.

88. Al-Bukhari # 3655.

89. Kitab-us-Sunnah of Ibn Abi Aasim.

prophethood and messengership, love of the Companions, and whatever else that falls under the criterion of these subjects, on account of the separationists therein declaring some among them to be disbelievers in contrast to the first type (i.e. Islamic Jurisprudence). Indeed they differ in that without neither takfir nor tafsiq (declaring one to be sinful) against the opponent therein. So the interpretation of the narration as pertains to the splitting of the Islamic nation returns to this (i.e. the second mentioned) type of differing.[90]

This makes clear that the type of differing intended is that which clashes with the fundamentals of the religion in which there is consensus as relates to apparent and hidden matters of the religion, in layman's terms in creed and physical acts of worship. These matters are dubbed the usool or fundamentals i.e. whatsoever the Islamic Nation has unanimous agreement therein from the time of the Companions until now regardless if the matter is from creed or worship. It is important to emphasize the key component in the definition, that being the unanimous agreement of the Islamic Nation; Generally with the first three generations of Muslim and more specific as pertains to the Companions.

IS THERE DIFFERING IN CREED?

We've seen that the differing as pertains to fiqh jurisprudence i.e. that which is connected to rulings on actions or how an act of worship is performed, relates to that which there is no consensus among the scholars; with respect to creed are there affairs among it where a consensus is nonexistent? The answer is yes there are affairs therein where a consensus is nonexistent. Thus, in this regard, the creed has two categories:

The Fundamental Aspects of Creed: This aspect is what differing as pertains to contradiction and opposition is affixed to, as it is to literally clash with aspects of the creed in which there is unequivocal proofs that dispels any doubt or foreign interpretation as relates to the intent. Consequently, he who differs in this aspect of creed can be judged to either be a disbeliever/apostate, deviant innovator, or misguided and astray.

---

90. تحفة الأحوذي شرح جامع الترمذي.

The Subsidiary Aspects of Creed: This aspect is where the text is not as clear and explicit as the first aspect resulting in scholars understanding the issue in different ways. It is the aspect of creed to which the differing in comprehension is affixed. Consequently the differing in this regard is not viewed to be that which threatens one's Islam or threatens one's ruling of being righteous, on the contrary it is as is detailed previously with respect to the types of differing.

To further elucidate this matter we have the speech of Sheikh Muhammad ibn Salih al-Uthaymin which effectively brings clarity to the matter. The Sheikh said:

> The reality is it is not possible for us to say that in every affair of creed there is unwavering certainty. This is because among the affairs of creed there is that which the scholars differ and whatsoever within it is differing among the people of knowledge it is not invariably certain. For example; the torment of the grave, does it befall the body or the soul? Additionally the scholars differ with regards to what is weighed; is it the actions, the scrolls (which contain the recorded account of actions), or he who implemented actions? Likewise the scholars differ with regards to the Garden in which Adam was lodged. Was it the everlasting Garden (i.e. paradise) or a garden in this world?
>
> Moreover they differ as relates to the Prophet ﷺ seeing his Lord. Did he see Allah with his eyes or with his heart? They differ as it pertains to the Hell-Fire, is it everlasting or temporal? All of these affairs are from creed, so the statement that there is no differing in creed unrestrictedly is incorrect.[91]

This point of Sheikh al-Uthaymin is of paramount importance, especially in light of what has been witnessed here in the US on account of ignorance in this issue. Unfortunately, ignorance as pertains to this subject has caused a stark imbalance among those who attribute themselves to the Sunnah in the west generally and in the US specifically. Rulings of innovation, partisanship, defense of partisanship, watering down the truth, waging war against the Sunnah, deficiency in knowledge, etc; are some of the remarks made on account of ignorance to this affair, all of which are unjustified and incorrect in light of the text and principles

---

91. Al-Aqeedah as-Safaariniyyah.

derived therefrom. However, the perpetrators of these rulings assume that they are defending the truth instead they are corrupting the masses' understanding of the issue, misrepresenting the Sunnah, oppressing their brothers with unwarranted attacks, and in most cases excommunicating their brothers in contrast to the principles and guidelines which command unity.

THE CONSEQUENCES FOR DIFFERING

Not only does Allah prohibit dysfunction and disunity among the Muslims, He also informs us of the consequences for falling into this prohibition. The negative ramifications are all encompassing and can easily be described as chaotic and catastrophic. This is no exaggeration when contemplating on the statement of Allah as relates to the consequences for disunity, as illustrated in the following:

$$ وَأَطِيعُوا۟ ٱللَّهَ وَرَسُولَهُۥ وَلَا تَنَـٰزَعُوا۟ فَتَفْشَلُوا۟ وَتَذْهَبَ رِيحُكُمْ وَٱصْبِرُوٓا۟ إِنَّ ٱللَّهَ مَعَ ٱلصَّـٰبِرِينَ $$

And obey Allah and His Messenger, and do not be at variance with one another lest you become emasculated and your strength departs. Be patient! Undoubtedly Allah is with the patient. [Al-Anfal: 46]

Imam Ibn Jarir At-Tabari said while commenting on the portion of the verse "..and do not be at variance with one another lest you become emasculated": "i.e., do not differ resulting in your separation and your hearts becoming divided 'lest you become emasculated' i.e., you become weak and cowardly."

He also said concerning the portion of the verse, "..and your strength departs": "The strength of the Messenger's companions diminished when they contradicted him (i.e. his command) during the battle of Uhud."[92]

Sheikh Muhammad al-Amin Ash-Shinqiti said:

---

92. Tafsir At-Tabari.

In this noble verse Allah prohibits the believers from falling into dispute (among each other) elucidating the fact that it is the cause of diminishment. Moreover, He prohibits division in other places, for instance His statement {And cling to the Rope of Allah altogether, and do not be divided...} Ali-Imran: 103, and similar to it from Quranic verses. As for His statement in this verse {..and your strength departs} i.e. your formidability, some scholars say your (divine) assistance.[93]

Disputation, division, excommunication, etc; are a means to the removal of blessings upon the Muslim nation and its consequences are widespread. Blessings i.e. barakah is defined as the continuity of divine related good within a thing, that continuity being credited to He Who is the true bestower of this good upon someone or within something. Among the blessings bestowed upon the Muslims is safety and security. This safety and security is removed as a result of division which in extreme cases has led to the spilling of blood, displacement from homes, destruction of property, exhausting of wealth, starvation, widespread panic, environmental and ecological ruin, etc. We have within the prophetic traditions examples of how good was lost on account of disputation and division, reflect on the following:

> *Ubadah ibn As-Samit said: "The Messenger صَلَّى اللهُ عَلَيْهِ وَسَلَّم came out to inform us about the night of al-Qadr, but two men from the Muslims were arguing. So he صَلَّى اللهُ عَلَيْهِ وَسَلَّم said, 'I came to inform you of the night of al-Qadr; however, so-and-so and so-and-so disputed so it (i.e. knowledge thereof) was taken away and perhaps that is better for you. Search for it during the seventh, ninth, and fifth day (i.e. of the last ten days of Ramadan).'"[94]*

Muslim in his authentic collection (1167) also conveys this narration from a chain of transmission emanating from Abu Saeed al-Khudri where the Prophet صَلَّى اللهُ عَلَيْهِ وَسَلَّم stated the following:

> *O people! Indeed it was made clear to me the night of al-Qadr and I have come out (from i'tikaf in the masjid) to inform you of it, then two men*

---

93. Adwaa-ul-Bayaan.

94. Al-Bukhari: 49.

came disputing and with them was the Shaitan, so I forgot it (i.e. its exact night), thus search for it during the last ten nights of Ramadan i.e., during the ninth, seventh, and fifth.

Al-Hafidh ibn Hajr al-Asqalaani quotes the speech of Al-Qadhi Iyyadh where he said:

> Within it (i.e. the narration) is evidence illustrating that quarreling is blameworthy. Likewise that disputation is the means to abstract punishment, in this case deprivation (i.e. knowledge was deprived). Also indicated within it is that any place in which the Shaitan is present, the blessings and good therein are removed.[95]

Imam An-Nawawi affirms this understanding in his statement: "Within it is clarification that the intent of taken away is the removal of its specific knowledge, and if removal of its existence was intended he ﷺ would not have ordered the searching for it." [96]

Although the example of the ill effects of disputation and division in this narration are clear, we have another example within the prophetic traditions. The following is collected by Imam al-Bukhari in his authentic collection (114):

> Abdullah ibn Abbas said: When the illness of the Prophet ﷺ worsened he said: 'Give me some writing material so that I may write that by which you shall not go astray thereafter.' Umar (then) said: 'Sickness has overwhelmed the Prophet ﷺ as we have with us Allah's book and it is sufficient.' Consequently they (i.e. the family of the Prophet) differed and there was an abundant uproar, so he ﷺ said: 'Leave me! It is not befitting that you dispute/argue in front of me.'"

Al Hafidh ibn Hajr al-Asqalaani said:

> Undoubtedly differing was the cause of the abandonment of writing. Likewise within the narration is evidence indicating the allowance of writing knowledge along with differing, oftentimes being the means to deprivation of good just like what occurred in the story about the two

---

95. Fath-ul-Bari.

96. Sharh Sahih Muslim.

men who disputed, resulting in the removal of (knowledge concerning) the specific night of al-Qadr.[97]

Ibn Abbas would say, when narrating this incident to others: "Indeed it was a calamity that Allah's Messenger ﷺ was obstructed from writing (i.e. his statement in that instance)."

Unfortunately, this is the cause for the removal of Allah's blessings on the Islamic Nation today and the apparent state of weakness that has befallen us, despite the fact that we are plentiful in numbers. Many among the Muslims recognize our dire conditions and desire rectification; however, they are totally ignorant as relates to the means of this rectification and act as if obfuscated when the actual causes to our low state is explained in clear and simple terms.

Nonetheless, the means to unity is clearly defined within the revelation, unfortunately with many Muslims suffering from emotionalism and shortsightedness, whenever the means to achieve unity and rectification of the Islamic Nation is detailed they reject the means in preference of their opinion based on irrationality and pointless fervor that continues the detrimental cycle of disunity and weakness throughout the earth. This is the sad reality we are faced with today, and Allah knows best. May Allah rectify our affairs.

---

97. Fath-ul-Bari.

The Third Principle

Author

Undoubtedly the—mechanism—that completes unity is the hearing and obeying whomever is charged with authority over us, even though he may be an ethiopian slave. So Allah illustrated this with an adequate and prevalent clarification with varying perspectives among the types of elucidations both legislatively (as relates to Islam) and predictably predetermined. Thereafter this fundamental became unfamiliar with an abundance of those who claim knowledge, so how then is it enacted?

Commentator

This principle alludes to a profound statement of Allah's Messenger ﷺ as pertains to submitting to the leadership of the Islamic Nation regardless of what title he is given e.g. king, president, sultan, khalifah, general, etc. If authority is placed in his hands then it is binding for the constituents to follow. The narration where the statement is mentioned is as follows:

> Al-Irbad ibn Sariyah said: One day we prayed with Allah's Messenger ﷺ thereafter he approached us and gave an intense admonition causing the eyes to flow with tears and the hearts to tremble. So an attendee said, "O Messenger of Allah! It is as if this admonition is a farewell, so what are you entrusting to us?" He ﷺ replied: "I advise you with taqwa of Allah, and to hear and obey even if it be to an Ethiopian slave. Undoubtedly whoever lives after me shall see an

abundance of differing, hence what is upon him is my Sunnah and that of the Rightly Guided Successors. Adhere to it and bite onto it with your molars. In addition, I caution you from novel matters (in the religion), for every novelty is an innovation, and every innovation is misguidance."[98]

Bukhari collects a narration (693, 696, 7142) similar in meaning which is reported by Anas ibn Malik and it is as follows: Allah's Messenger ﷺ said: "Hear and obey even if an Ethiopian slave whose head is like a raisin is granted authority over you."

In the authentic collection of Muslim (648) it states: Abu Dharr said: "My close friend (referring to the Messenger ﷺ) advised me to listen and obey even if it be a maimed slave."

It is understood from these narrations that submission to the Muslim authority is an obligation upon his constituents, for this reason the Prophet ﷺ used extreme examples to illustrate this obligation, specifically the example of a slave, he who is owned himself. Imam an-Nawawi said: "The intent is the least in value of the slaves, in other words, listen and adhere to the commander even if he is from the lowest of lineages and even if he is a slave being extremely dark (in complexion) and amputated; obedience to him is still obligatory."

Shams-ul-Haqq al-Atheem Abaadi quotes Imam al-Khitabi as saying,

He intends by this example obedience to whoever is granted authority as commander over you, although he may be an Ethiopian slave. He did not intend for the commander to be an Ethiopian slave on account of it being firmly reported that he ﷺ said 'The leaders are from the Quraish' so he put forth a similitude as pertains to a specific thing that would not be valid if it existed, similar to his ﷺ statement, 'Whoever builds a masjid for Allah's sake even if it is like the sparrow's nest, Allah will build for him a house in paradise.' So the size of a sparrow's nest cannot be (suitable as) a masjid for a human being and the equivalent of this type of speech is plentiful.[99]

---

98. Abu Dawud: 4607.

99. Awn-ul-Ma'bood.

WAS PROPHET MUHAMMAD RACIST?

Attention: There should be no thought in the minds of the Muslim based on this narration that the Prophet ﷺ was racist or had any traits of racism within him. Furthermore, the commentary of Imam An-Nawawi concerning the complexion of the leader is not something derived from the narration, but is from his own interpretation. Likewise what is not accurately deduced from the narration is that Ethiopians are of a low lineage as these are Imam An-Nawawi's assumptions. On the contrary, what is understood is the importance of hearing and obeying by usage of an exaggerated example of a slave being in authority notwithstanding the fact that he is maimed or amputated which would be undesirable regardless of which ethnicity he may be, whether Arab or non Arab. The Quran teaches us that no matter how dark one is in complexion or how light he may be, all are a sign for the magnificence, power, knowledge, ability, and perfection of the Creator of man, this is illustrated in the following:

$$\text{وَمِنْ ءَايَٰتِهِۦ خَلْقُ ٱلسَّمَٰوَٰتِ وَٱلْأَرْضِ وَٱخْتِلَٰفُ أَلْسِنَتِكُمْ وَأَلْوَٰنِكُمْ ۚ إِنَّ فِى ذَٰلِكَ لَأَيَٰتٍ لِّلْعَٰلِمِينَ}$$

And from His signs is the creation of the heavens and earth and the differences in your languages and your complexions. Surely, in that are signs for men of sound knowledge. [Ar-Rum: 22]

Ibn Kathir said:

> The differentiation of their complexions is their ornamentation. So, all of the inhabitants of earth, rather all of the inhabitants of this worldly life since Allah created Adam till the establishment of the Hour all have two eyes, two eye brows, a nose, a forehead, a mouth, and two cheeks and no one among them looks identical to another.

Imam al-Qurtubi said:

> The differentiation of complexion with respect to their images i.e., white, black, and red. Thus you will not see anyone except that you are able to differentiate between him and another. Moreover, these things are not on account of actions of sperm, nor due to actions of

the parent, thus it is a must for a doer (to this differentiation). So, it is known that the doer is Allah the Exalted; and this is the most evident proof pointing to the Regulator (of affairs), The Originator.

In layman's terms, the varying races and complexions indicate the perfection of the Creator and His ability as He is the one that fashions the face and shape of man. When looking at any particular race Allah has made for each race features specific to it; however, each individual is distinguishable from the other and are not identical. For example, the black race are brown complected people. Brown ranging from the darkest (i.e. darker than the color of chocolate) to the lightest, having similar shaped noses, lips, etc. However, Allah has fashioned their faces making distinctions between one person and another of the same race with shared features. This has been done with billions of people as pertains to one race. Therefore is this not a sign for Allah's grandeur?!

Unfortunately, among the modern Christian attacks against Islam and its Prophet is that he was a racist. Usage of the previously mentioned authentic narration is among the utterly pathetic attempts at substantiating these claims while negating what the narration actually intends. The allegations against our Prophet Muhammad ﷺ are easily disproved when considering several apparent and clear factors. First, what is racism? The following are definitions of the term racism:

- A belief or doctrine that inherent differences among the various human racial groups determine cultural or individual achievement, usually involving the idea that one's own race is superior and has the right to dominate others or that a particular racial group is inferior to the others.
- A belief that race is a fundamental determinant of human traits and capacities and that racial differences produce an inherent superiority of a particular race.
- Behavior or attitudes that reflect and foster the belief of racial discrimination or prejudice.
- The belief that people of some races are inferior to others, and the behavior which is the result of this belief.
- Prejudice, antagonism, or discrimination by an individual,

institution, or society, against a person or people on the basis of their nationality or race.

The person that holds such ideas and manifests it in behavior is a racist. This is a characteristic that is impossible to attribute to the Prophet Muhammad ﷺ despite the futile attempts by modern Christian propagandists that deceptively interpret authentic narrations to substantiate farfetched and delusional allegations of this nature. Second, the teachings of our Prophet ﷺ dispel the claim of racism, Arab supremacy or nationalism, etc. If they truly believe this claim of racism, then how is it that it cannot be substantiated by his ﷺ teachings? The following are some examples of such:

Abu Huraira quotes Allah's Messenger ﷺ statement: "Undoubtedly Allah does not look to neither your outward appearances nor wealth, on the contrary He looks to your hearts and actions."[100]

This narration indicates that no one's outward appearance regardless if he is fat or skinny, tall or short, black or white, etc; has any bearing on obtaining mercy, forgiveness, and reward from Him, nor in being brought close to Him. In contrast to sincerity of the heart and actions congruent to Allah's revelation as these things bring a person closer to Allah, and on account of these things the servant with purity of heart and actions obtains reward.

Abu Nadhra narrates the Prophet's ﷺ statement: "O people! Your Lord is one, your father is one, thus there is no virtue with the Arab over the non Arab nor the non Arab over the Arab. Likewise, not for the white over the black nor the black over the white except with regards to taqwa. Have I conveyed (i.e. the message)?..."[101]

---

100. Muslim: 34.

101. Ahmad: 23489.

Abu Dharr reports Allah's Messenger's ﷺ statement: "Look! Surely you are not better than neither a white person nor a black unless you surpass him in taqwa."[102]

These narrations are sufficient in definitively illustrating the core teachings of the Prophet ﷺ and disproving the claims of Christian propagandists that allege racism from him. Although they attempt to justify this claim from varying means, this commentary is only a summary in rebuttal of the paramount claim. Unfortunately this work is not for the purpose of responding to the intricacies of their claims; however, it is hoped that Allah will grant me success in addressing their claims in a detailed manner in a future article or book by His permission. I ask Allah for success in that regard.

THE FOUNDATION WITH THE MUSLIM HEAD OF STATE IS TO HEAR AND OBEY

The following is a presentation of some of the evidence which supports the fact that the fundamental ruling as relates to the Muslim leader is obedience. These evidences are invariable in their meaning as they clearly illustrate this important point. Allah says:

يَٰٓأَيُّهَا ٱلَّذِينَ ءَامَنُوٓاْ أَطِيعُواْ ٱللَّهَ وَأَطِيعُواْ ٱلرَّسُولَ وَأُوْلِي ٱلْأَمْرِ مِنكُمْ ۖ فَإِن تَنَٰزَعْتُمْ فِي شَيْءٍ فَرُدُّوهُ إِلَى ٱللَّهِ وَٱلرَّسُولِ إِن كُنتُمْ تُؤْمِنُونَ بِٱللَّهِ وَٱلْيَوْمِ ٱلْآخِرِ ۚ ذَٰلِكَ خَيْرٌ وَأَحْسَنُ تَأْوِيلًا

O you who believe! Obey Allah, obey the Messenger, and those in authority over you. If you all differ in a matter, then refer it back to Allah and His Messenger if you believe in Allah and the Last Day. That is good and better in terms of interpretation. [An-Nisa: 59]

---

102. Sahih Al-Jami: 1505.

The erudite scholars of exegesis differ on the interpretation of "and those in authority over you" and their opinions in this regard are as follows:

- The leader or head of state over the Muslims i.e. president, king, prime minister, khalifah, amir, sultan, etc.
- The people of knowledge i.e. the scholars of the Islamic Nation.
- The leader or head of state over the Muslims along with the erudite scholars of the Islamic Nation.
- The Companions of the Prophet specifically.
- Abu Bakr and Umar specifically among the Companions.

Imam An-Nawawi said:

> The scholars state that the intent of "those in authority" is whomever Allah has made binding obedience towards as relates to the leaders and heads of state. This is the position of the majority of scholars among the (pious) predecessors and successors (of the predecessors) from among the experts of exegesis, erudite Islamic jurists, and others. Moreover it is alleged that they are the scholars, likewise it is said that they are both the heads of state and the scholars. As for whoever says they are the Companions exclusively, surely he has erred.[103]

Although there exists several opinions on this matter, the correct opinion seems distinguished from the remainder of opinions. That being that its intent is the leaders or heads of state, as the authentic narrations indicate this explicitly. Imam Ash-Shawkani said:

> They are the leaders, rulers, judges, and everyone that has Islamically Legislative authority not a polytheistic related authority. Thus the intent is obedience in whatever they command and forbid as long as it (i.e. the command) is not (to commit) sinful acts, as there is no obedience to a created being if it is disobedience to the Creator just as it is authentically attributed to him. In contrast, Jabir ibn Abdullah, Mujahid, Malik, and Ad-dahak said those in authority are the people of knowledge and the Quran. It is reported that Mujahid held the opinion that they are Muhammad's Companions. Kaisan said they are the people of intellect and rationale. The more preponderant speech is the first.[104]

---

103. Sharh Sahih Muslim.

104. Fath-ul-Qadeer.

The following are authentic narrations that make clear the fact that the leaders/rulers are intended by "those in authority":

Abu Huraira narrated from the Prophet ﷺ stating that he said: "Whoever obeyed me has surely obeyed Allah and whoever disobeys me has disobeyed Allah. Furthermore whoever obeys the ruler has obeyed me and whoever disobeys the ruler has disobeyed me."[105]

Abdullah ibn Umar stated; I heard Allah's Messenger ﷺ say: "Whoever removes his hand from obedience (i.e. to the ruler), he shall meet Allah on the day of resurrection having no excuse for himself. Moreover, whoever dies and there is no (rope of) allegiance around his neck then he dies a death in the state of ignorance."[106]

Abdullah ibn Abbas narrates the Prophet ﷺ as saying: "Whoever hates something from his leader then let him be patient, and whoever departs from (in terms of obedience) the leader by a handspan, then he dies a state of ignorance type death."[107]

Salamah ibn Yazid al-Ju'fi said: O Prophet of Allah! If you were to see the leaders stand among us demanding from us their rights while preventing ours' then what would you command? He ﷺ shunned him, so he asked again a second and third time. Then al-Ash'ab ibn Qais pulled him aside resulting in him ﷺ saying, "Listen and obey, indeed the burden they've been made to bear is upon them and what you've been made to bear is upon you."[108]

Abu Hurairah narrates the Prophet ﷺ as saying: "The Descendants of Israel used to be ruled by prophets. Everytime a prophet passed on another succeeded him. Undoubtedly there will be no prophet after me; however, there will be successors in abundance." They said: So What do you command us with? He ﷺ replied: "Fulfill your pledges to them one after the other, and give them their rights as Allah

---

105. Bukhari: 7137 and Muslim: 1835.

106. Muslim: 1851.

107. Bukhari: 7053.

108. Muslim: 1846.

surely will ask them about their constituency (i.e. those under their authority)."[109]

Ubadah ibn Samit quotes Allah's Messenger ﷺ as saying: "Whoever worships Allah without associating a partner in worship with Him, performs the prayer, pays the zakah, and hears and obeys (the leadership); Allah will most certainly enter him into paradise from any of its gates. Surely it has eight gates."[110]

These narrations unequivocally demonstrate the obligation to follow, obey, and comply with the orders of the ruler (in a manner not particularized for the scholars). This is the fundamental ruling in this regard thus whoever opposes it has opposed Allah and His Messenger ﷺ. Al-Hafidh ibn Hajr al-Asqalaani said:

> This sentence—i.e. Whoever obeys me has obeyed Allah—is derived from the Exalted's statement: **"Whoever obeys the Messenger has obeyed Allah,"** [An-Nisaa: 80] i.e. because I don't order with anything except that which Allah orders. Consequently whoever implements what I command, obeys He who ordered me to give the command. Furthermore it is possible for its meaning to be because Allah ordered obedience to me so whoever obeys me undoubtedly obeys the command of Allah to obey me."[111]

Although submission to the ruler is the fundamental position, it doesn't mean this submission is unrestricted. On the contrary, compliance to any order issued is contingent on it being in accordance with that which Allah loves and is pleased with. In other words, if a command is issued and it is considered to be disobedience to Allah, then it is forbidden to comply with such an order while still generally being in a state of compliance to the ruler's overall authority. The following authentic narrations elucidate this point:

---

109. Bukhari: 3455 and Muslim: 1842.

110. Kitab-us-Sunnah of Ibn Abi Asim: 1027.

111. Fath-ul-Bari.

Abdullah ibn Umar narrated that the Prophet ﷺ said: "Upon a Muslim man is the hearing and obeying as pertains to what he loves and hates unless he is ordered to commit disobedience. If he is ordered to commit disobedience then there is neither hearing nor obedience."[112]

Ali ibn Abi Talib said: Allah's Messenger ﷺ dispatched a detachment and appointed a man from the Ansar as operations leader over them. He instructed them to hear and obey (i.e. the leader). As a result they eventually vexed him in an affair, so he said to them, "gather firewood for me" and they gathered it for him. Then he said, "ignite a fire" so they ignited a fire. He then said, "Did not Allah's Messenger ﷺ instruct you to listen to and obey me?" They replied in the affirmative, so he said "Then enter it (i.e. the fire)." As a result the people looked towards one another and said, "We have fled towards Allah's Messenger away from the fire—i.e. Refusing to comply with his order— and they remained upon this position. Eventually his anger subsided and the fire became extinguished. So when they returned to the Prophet ﷺ they mentioned what transpired. On account of that he said, "If they had entered it, they would not have exited it. Obedience is only in that which is good."[113]

Sheikh Muhammad Nasiruddin al-Albani said:

An abundance of benefit is found within this narration, the most important of them is that obedience to anyone in terms of it being disobedience to Allah is not permissible. Regardless if obedience is given to the ruler, scholar, or highly proficient teachers (of Islamic Sciences).[114]

Sheikh Muhammad Amin Ash-Shinqeeti commenting on An-Nisaa: 59 said:

Allah repeats the verb—obey—in connection with Allah and the Messenger ﷺ but doesn't repeat it with regards to those in authority, that's because obedience to them is not an independent matter. On the contrary, it is in conformity with Allah and His

---

112. Muslim: 1839.

113. Muslim: 1840(a).

114. Silsilah As-Sahihah, commentary to hadith 181.

Messenger's ﷺ obedience just as is found in the narration, "There is no obedience to the creation in terms of disobedience to the Creator."

DOES OBEDIENCE APPLY TO AN OPENLY SINFUL AND OPPRESSIVE RULER?

This issue is one of the dilemmas of contemporary times on account of the spreading of ignorance and religious verdicts which contradict revelation. There is no doubt that contemporary leadership over Muslims in multiple lands are of less quality, in terms of implementation of Allah's religion upon themselves first and ordering it upon their constituents, than their predecessors who lived centuries before them. However, despite the reduction in uprightness among them we still have revelation to abide by in terms of our relationship and conduct with them. Hence, even if the leadership is outwardly sinful and oppressive the text clearly establishes the fulfillment of listening and obeying despite their shortcomings. The following narrations illustrate this point explicitly:

> *Awf ibn Malik narrates the statement of Allah's Messenger ﷺ when he said: "The best of your leaders are those whom you love and they love you. They pray for you and you pray for them. The worst of your leaders are those whom you hate and they hate you. You curse them and they curse you." So someone said: O Messenger of Allah! Should we not rebel against them with the sword? He ﷺ replied: "No not while they organize the establishment of prayer among you. Whenever you see something from the leadership causing you to hate him, then hate his action; however, do not remove your hands from (overall) obedience."[115]*

Ponder on the circumstance of the worst leaders to whom the Messenger ﷺ informs us. Their circumstance will be to the degree that people will hold hatred for them and literally curse them. Thus is it assumed that leaders of this nature are anywhere near being upon righteousness similar to Abu Bakr and Umar?! If these leaders hate and curse their own constituency is it fathomable that they act justly with them?! It would

---

115. Muslim: 1855.

be unfathomable to believe that these types of rulers do not merit the hatred held within the hearts of their constituency as the remainder of the narration indicates as relates to seeking permission to rebel. Despite this the Prophet ﷺ did not make the revolting against them permissible, on the contrary he encouraged the maintaining of obedience.

Imam An-Nawawi said about a narration whose wording is slightly different but meaning is identical to the aforementioned: As for his ﷺ speech, "Should we not fight them? He ﷺ replied, 'No as long as they pray'" this indicates the meaning of what preceded that being the prohibition of revolting against the leaders on account of oppression and sinfulness exclusively while they have not altered anything from the foundations of Islam.

Hudaifah ibn al-Yaman quotes the Prophet ﷺ when he said: "There will be after me rulers who neither are guided by my guidance nor do they adopt my traditions. Situated among them will be men, their hearts are that of devils within the body of a human. I (Hudaifah) said 'How should I behave O Messenger of Allah ﷺ if I come across this?' He ﷺ said 'Hear and obey the leader even if he smites your neck and seizes your property (i.e. wealth).'"[116]

Adi ibn Hatim said: O Messenger of Allah ﷺ we're not asking about obedience to the pious (ruler), on the contrary we're asking about he who does this and that (he consequently mentions evil acts)? So he replied: "Fear Allah, and listen and obey."[117]

To reiterate, the Prophet ﷺ gave an explicitly negative description of these tyrannical rulers i.e., hearts of devils within human bodies, and even mentioned atrocities that they will commit against their constituency; despite that the instruction to hear and obey is equally clear.

---

116. Muslim: 1847.

117. Kitab-us-Sunnah of Ibn Abi Asim: 1069.

WHEN IS REMOVAL OF OBEDIENCE AND REVOLT JUSTIFIED?

Although the fundamental rule with regards to leadership and governance of the Islamic Nation is obedience to the ruler/leader and prohibition from removing one's hand from obedience to him, there are exceptions to that rule. If there arises a circumstance that merits removal of obedience and revolt then in that instance revolt is permissible. This is illustrated by the following narration:

> *Ubadah ibn Samit said: "Allah's Messenger ﷺ summoned us resulting in us pledging allegiance to him. Among that which he imposed upon us was hearing and obeying (i.e. the ruler) as pertains to what was pleasurable or displeasurable, in adversity and prosperity, and when preference is given to other than us. Also to not contest the authority of he who is in office (i.e. of leadership and governance) unless you see unequivocal disbelief to which there is undeniable evidence with you granted by Allah."[118]*

Sheikh Muhammad Nasiruddin al-Albani when asked about unequivocal disbelief answered by saying:

> It is flagrant disbelief in which the carrier of it has proof to which he himself is convinced (i.e. of his disbelief) aside from being able to persuade others of it. Thus proof here is glaringly obvious and unmistakably noticeable insomuch that he comes with proof legitimizing the disbelief. As for if he comes with proof that he is persuaded by, then revolt against the ruler is not permissible on account of it being in opposition to our commission (i.e. as constituents giving the pledge to hear and obey) and our (factually) known (i.e. of his condition).[119]

In light of this there are several things that must be highlighted as pertains to unequivocal disbelief, and they are as follows:

- The action is unanimously agreed to be disbelief i.e. not an affair in which there is differing concerning the action; is it disbelief or a major sin, etc.
- The action leaves no room for interpretation insomuch that

---

118. Muslim: 1840.

119. Jami Turath, vol. 5.

one has to delve into the circumstance to derive if the case of disbelief is valid or not.

- The action is well known among the Muslims to be disbelief, even among the commoner with minimal to no real education concerning Allah's religion insomuch that even the perpetrator of the action is well aware that it is disbelief.

For this reason Sheikh al-Albani said within the same verdict above:

We give justification with the trial of Mamoon al-Abbasi when he separated from the Islamic world during his reign by way of his statement that the Quran is created. The Islamic world at the time, which was composed of luminary scholars in the fields of hadith science and fiqh jurisprudence, did not rebel against their government. Additionally there is no doubt that they were stronger than we are today as pertains to (having ability to) revolt; however, when they based their ruling—i.e. Forbidding the Muslims from rebelling against their leadership unless they saw unequivocal disbelief—they did not observe unequivocal disbelief, in terms of being possible for us to understand by way of an expression that some scholars use occasionally, that being it (i.e. unequivocal disbelief) is well known by way of the religion, by necessity. In other words it is a ruling in which a particular and general aspect of people share as pertains to awareness; the scholar and the ignoramus. Hence, if the leader publicly manifests a matter definitely prohibited from the religion by necessity, in this instance the pledge of allegiance is discontinued on account of him committing unequivocal disbelief.[120]

Unfortunately, this affair—i.e. Rebelling against the ruler with justification of disbelief—many among the Muslims are intensely preoccupied. However, they approach these affairs without understanding the precepts and principles surrounding this affair. Likewise without comprehension of the circumstance of the leadership as pertains to why certain things are allowed or not allowed, along with a thorough understanding of the leader's authoritative abilities especially in light of the emergence of Muslim countries with secular governments. As a result, moves are made that contradict the goals of the perfect Islamic

---

120. Jami Turath, vol. 5.

Legislation whose outcomes are totally undesirable and catastrophic, as observed throughout the Islamic world today.

THE PREREQUISITES FOR REVOLT AGAINST A MUSLIM GOVERNMENT

A prerequisite in the Islamic technical sense has a two part definition and it is that which does not necessitate by way of its presence the existence of what is contingent upon it, also it is that which necessitates by way of its absence, the absence of what is contingent upon it. This is applicable to acts of worship in terms of its validity or futility. In order to better understand its intent it's important to examine both components of the definition.

"That which necessitates by way of its absence, the absence of what is contingent upon it." This is the second component of the definition and its meaning is straightforward. The portion "what is contingent upon it" is the act of worship itself. The prerequisite must be in place prior to embarking on its performance, thus if it is absent the act of worship likewise is absent in terms of validity and acceptance. For example the prayer is an act of worship contingent upon ritual purification, i.e. ritual purity is a prerequisite for the validity of the prayer; thus if one prays while not being in the state of ritual purity the prayer is invalid. Furthermore, it is important to mention that the prerequisite is not part of the act of worship but must be in place for the act to be performed.

"That which does not necessitate by way of its presence the existence of what is contingent upon it." This component is also straightforward in its implication. It refers to the prerequisite being in place; however, the existence of the prerequisite doesn't mean that the act of worship exists also, why? Because the act of worship now must be performed. This point must be emphasized i.e. the prerequisite not being part of the act of worship. For this reason a prerequisite to an act of worship can be present while the act of worship itself is not, because it has yet to be performed. This is also applicable in a case where an act of worship has more than one prerequisite. In other words an act of worship could have two prerequisites yet only one is available, thus the act of worship can't be performed unless all of the prerequisites are present.

The scholars of Islam have outlined the prerequisites needed in order for the removal of obedience to be permissible. Each prerequisite has support from the text and they illustrate the proper circumstance required that changes the base rule from prohibition to permissible due to that specific circumstance being that which produces an absolute or preponderant benefit to the overall community. The following are the prerequisites required:

FIRST PREREQUISITE: THE MANIFESTATION OF UNEQUIVOCAL DISBELIEF

This prerequisite, its evidence, and its meaning has been explained previously thus there is no need to be repetitive in this regard.

SECOND PREREQUISITE: THE ABILITY TO REMOVE THE AUTHORITY

The ability to perform an act of worship encompasses the entirety of the religion. Consequently if a person is placed in a circumstance where he is inadequate with regards to fulfillment of a highly recommended or obligatory act, then the responsibility is either dropped or lessened in that particular case. The following are some of the evidence for this prerequisite.

فَٱتَّقُوا۟ ٱللَّهَ مَا ٱسْتَطَعْتُمْ

Fear Allah in accordance with your ability. [At-Taghabun: 16]

لَا يُكَلِّفُ ٱللَّهُ نَفْسًا إِلَّا وُسْعَهَا ۚ لَهَا مَا كَسَبَتْ وَعَلَيْهَا مَا ٱكْتَسَبَتْ ۗ رَبَّنَا لَا تُؤَاخِذْنَآ إِن نَّسِينَآ أَوْ أَخْطَأْنَا ۚ رَبَّنَا وَلَا تَحْمِلْ عَلَيْنَآ إِصْرًا كَمَا حَمَلْتَهُۥ عَلَى ٱلَّذِينَ مِن قَبْلِنَا ۚ رَبَّنَا وَلَا تُحَمِّلْنَا مَا لَا طَاقَةَ لَنَا بِهِۦ ۖ وَٱعْفُ عَنَّا وَٱغْفِرْ لَنَا وَٱرْحَمْنَآ ۚ أَنتَ مَوْلَىٰنَا فَٱنصُرْنَا عَلَى ٱلْقَوْمِ ٱلْكَٰفِرِينَ

Allah does not burden a soul beyond its capability. It's rewarded for what it earns (i.e. of good) and is requited for what it earns (i.e. of evil). "Our Lord! Do not bring us to account if we forget or make a mistake. Our Lord! Do not place a burden on us like You placed it on those that came before us. Our Lord! Do not place on us a burden greater than we have strength to bear. Pardon us, forgive us, and have mercy on us. You are our Maula so grant us victory over the disbelieving people. [Al Baqarah: 286]

لِيُنفِقْ ذُو سَعَةٍ مِّن سَعَتِهِۦ وَمَن قُدِرَ عَلَيْهِ رِزْقُهُۥ فَلْيُنفِقْ مِمَّآ ءَاتَىٰهُ ٱللَّهُ لَا يُكَلِّفُ ٱللَّهُ نَفْسًا إِلَّا مَآ ءَاتَىٰهَا سَيَجْعَلُ ٱللَّهُ بَعْدَ عُسْرٍ يُسْرًا

So the wealthy individual must spend according to his means, likewise the one whose resources are restricted must spend in accordance with what Allah has given him. Allah does not burden a soul beyond what He has given it, and Allah will grant ease after difficulty. [At-Talaq: 7]

Additionally we have within the authentic traditions of the Prophet ﷺ explicit statements that reinforce this point. They are as follows:

Abu Saeed al-Khudri narrated the statement of Allah's Messenger ﷺ when he said: "Whoever sees an evil then let him change it with his hand, if he is unable then with his tongue, if he is unable then with his heart; and that is the weakest of faith."[121]

Abu Hurairah quotes Allah's Messenger ﷺ as having said: "Leave me where I have left you, as those that came prior to you were only destroyed as a result of questioning and differing with their prophets. Thus whenever I forbid a matter then avoid it, and whenever I order you all to do something then implement it in accordance with your ability."[122]

---

121. Muslim: 49.

122. Bukhari: 7288 and Muslim: 1337.

Imran ibn Husayn quotes the Prophet ﷺ as saying to him: "Pray standing. If you are unable, then (pray) sitting. If you are unable then (pray) on your side."[123]

This textual evidence and whatever resembles them in meaning are what the principle "The Obligation Is Connected to One's Ability" is derived from. Sheikh Abdur Rahman ibn Nasir Sa'di said,

> Every individual who is incapable of implementing something from the prerequisites or obligations of the prayer has the responsibility dropped resulting in him praying according to his ability with respect to its requirements. Also whoever is unable to fast, having an unending disability e.g., a senior citizen or a sick person with an irreversible condition, breaks the fast and expiates by feeding a poor person each day (i.e., of the month). As for whoever is sick with an ailment that will eventually dissipate or is traveling—such a person—completes the number of days (missed while sick or on a journey) when the excuse to not implement the fast ends. Additionally the person unable to make the pilgrimage due to defect of the body, if he expects its ending then he remains patient until it ends; however, if it—is a defect—not expected to subside then a representative for him makes the pilgrimage in his place i.e., on his behalf.[124]

THIRD PREREQUISITE: A WORSE CIRCUMSTANCE DOES NOT RESULT FROM REBELLION

This prerequisite is based on several powerful principles within the religion. Among these principles are "The Consequence of Actions is What's Examined" and "If Two Corrupt/Harmful Circumstances (or things) Compete Implement The Least in Harm" which are examples that highlight the underlying goal of the perfect Islamic Legislation; that being to achieve benefit, advantages, and overall well being for the Islamic Nation and repel harms, disadvantages, and widespread corruption among it. These principles—like all within the religion— are derived directly from the text and illustrate Islam's suitability and compatibility in every time and place.

---

123. Bukhari: 1117.

124. Al-Qawaa'id wal Usool al-Jami'ah.

The following text is that from which these principles are derived.

يَسْـَٔلُونَكَ عَنِ ٱلشَّهْرِ ٱلْحَرَامِ قِتَالٍ فِيهِ ۖ قُلْ قِتَالٌ فِيهِ كَبِيرٌ ۖ وَصَدٌّ عَن سَبِيلِ ٱللَّهِ وَكُفْرٌ بِهِۦ وَٱلْمَسْجِدِ ٱلْحَرَامِ وَإِخْرَاجُ أَهْلِهِۦ مِنْهُ أَكْبَرُ عِندَ ٱللَّهِ ۚ وَٱلْفِتْنَةُ أَكْبَرُ مِنَ ٱلْقَتْلِ ۗ وَلَا يَزَالُونَ يُقَٰتِلُونَكُمْ حَتَّىٰ يَرُدُّوكُمْ عَن دِينِكُمْ إِنِ ٱسْتَطَٰعُوا ۚ وَمَن يَرْتَدِدْ مِنكُمْ عَن دِينِهِۦ فَيَمُتْ وَهُوَ كَافِرٌ فَأُولَٰٓئِكَ حَبِطَتْ أَعْمَٰلُهُمْ فِى ٱلدُّنْيَا وَٱلْآخِرَةِ ۖ وَأُولَٰٓئِكَ أَصْحَٰبُ ٱلنَّارِ ۖ هُمْ فِيهَا خَٰلِدُونَ

"They ask you about the prohibited months and fighting therein; say 'Fighting therein is a great transgression, but greater than that with Allah is hindrance from Allah's Path, disbelief in Him, blockage from access to Al Masjid Al Haram and expelling its people.' So strife/calamity is worse than killing." [Al-Baqarah: 217]

Imam al-Qurtubi said:

> The meaning of the verse with the majority of scholars is; undoubtedly you disbelievers of Quraish you hold it important to fight us during the prohibited month and what you do by obstructing from Allah's path for whoever wants Islam. Also your disbelief in Allah, your expulsion of the people from the masjid just as you did with Allah's Messenger ﷺ and his Companions, all of this is greater in magnitude with Allah as a crime."[125]

Thus what is understood is that physical confrontation and clashes during the prohibited months is evil and forbidden by Allah; however, the crimes of the Quraish outlined in the verse were of greater magnitude as pertains to evil, mischief, and corruption. So Allah ordered the lesser of the two evils to repel the graver evil. So the implementation of taking the least of two harmful circumstances was directly derived from this and other textual evidence similar in context. The following is another example:

---

125. Al-Jami' li Ihkam Al-Quran.

فَٱنطَلَقَا حَتَّىٰٓ إِذَا رَكِبَا فِى ٱلسَّفِينَةِ خَرَقَهَا ۚ قَالَ أَخَرَقْتَهَا لِتُغْرِقَ أَهْلَهَا لَقَدْ جِئْتَ شَيْـًٔا إِمْرًا ﴿٧١﴾ قَالَ أَلَمْ أَقُلْ إِنَّكَ لَن تَسْتَطِيعَ مَعِىَ صَبْرًا ﴿٧٢﴾ قَالَ لَا تُؤَاخِذْنِى بِمَا نَسِيتُ وَلَا تُرْهِقْنِى مِنْ أَمْرِى عُسْرًا ﴿٧٣﴾ فَٱنطَلَقَا حَتَّىٰٓ إِذَا لَقِيَا غُلَٰمًا فَقَتَلَهُ قَالَ أَقَتَلْتَ نَفْسًا زَكِيَّةًۢ بِغَيْرِ نَفْسٍ لَّقَدْ جِئْتَ شَيْـًٔا نُّكْرًا ﴿٧٤﴾ ۞ قَالَ أَلَمْ أَقُل لَّكَ إِنَّكَ لَن تَسْتَطِيعَ مَعِىَ صَبْرًا ﴿٧٥﴾ قَالَ إِن سَأَلْتُكَ عَن شَىْءٍۭ بَعْدَهَا فَلَا تُصَٰحِبْنِى ۖ قَدْ بَلَغْتَ مِن لَّدُنِّى عُذْرًا ﴿٧٦﴾ فَٱنطَلَقَا حَتَّىٰٓ إِذَآ أَتَيَآ أَهْلَ قَرْيَةٍ ٱسْتَطْعَمَآ أَهْلَهَا فَأَبَوْا أَن يُضَيِّفُوهُمَا فَوَجَدَا فِيهَا جِدَارًا يُرِيدُ أَن يَنقَضَّ فَأَقَامَهُ ۖ قَالَ لَوْ شِئْتَ لَتَّخَذْتَ عَلَيْهِ أَجْرًا ﴿٧٧﴾ قَالَ هَٰذَا فِرَاقُ بَيْنِى وَبَيْنِكَ ۚ سَأُنَبِّئُكَ بِتَأْوِيلِ مَا لَمْ تَسْتَطِع عَّلَيْهِ صَبْرًا ﴿٧٨﴾ أَمَّا ٱلسَّفِينَةُ فَكَانَتْ لِمَسَٰكِينَ يَعْمَلُونَ فِى ٱلْبَحْرِ فَأَرَدتُّ أَنْ أَعِيبَهَا وَكَانَ وَرَآءَهُم مَّلِكٌ يَأْخُذُ كُلَّ سَفِينَةٍ غَصْبًا ﴿٧٩﴾ وَأَمَّا ٱلْغُلَٰمُ فَكَانَ أَبَوَاهُ مُؤْمِنَيْنِ فَخَشِينَآ أَن يُرْهِقَهُمَا طُغْيَٰنًا وَكُفْرًا ﴿٨٠﴾ فَأَرَدْنَآ أَن يُبْدِلَهُمَا رَبُّهُمَا خَيْرًا مِّنْهُ زَكَوٰةً وَأَقْرَبَ رُحْمًا ﴿٨١﴾ وَأَمَّا ٱلْجِدَارُ فَكَانَ لِغُلَٰمَيْنِ يَتِيمَيْنِ فِى ٱلْمَدِينَةِ وَكَانَ تَحْتَهُ كَنزٌ لَّهُمَا وَكَانَ أَبُوهُمَا صَٰلِحًا فَأَرَادَ رَبُّكَ أَن يَبْلُغَآ أَشُدَّهُمَا وَيَسْتَخْرِجَا كَنزَهُمَا رَحْمَةً مِّن رَّبِّكَ ۚ وَمَا فَعَلْتُهُ عَنْ أَمْرِى ۚ ذَٰلِكَ تَأْوِيلُ مَا لَمْ تَسْطِع عَّلَيْهِ صَبْرًا ﴿٨٢﴾

So they departed (i.e., Musa and Khidr) until—at some point—they rode a boat and Khidr scuttled it. Musa said: 'Have you scuttled it in order to drown its people? You have come with a dreadfully evil act.' He (Khidr) replied: 'Did I not tell you that you wouldn't be able to be patient with me?' Musa said: 'Do not call me to account due to what I forgot and do not be difficult with me as concerns my affair.' So they departed till they met a boy to whom Khidr killed. Musa (reacting to what he witnessed) said: 'You have killed an innocent boy?! Surely you have committed an evil act!' Khidr said: Did I not tell you that you would have no patience with me?' Musa said: 'If I ask any question after this then do not keep me in your company. Indeed you have received an excuse from me.' Then they departed till they came to a town's people and requested food, yet they refused to entertain them. Thereafter they found within the town a wall on the verge of collapsing so Khidr set it up straight. Musa (then) said: 'If you wanted you could have taken wages for it.' Khidr then said: 'This is the parting between me and you, and I will inform you about the interpretation concerning that which you were impatient.' 'As for the boat it belonged to working class poor people who worked in the sea. Hence I wanted to cause a defect therein as there was a king behind them who seized all boats forcibly.' 'As for the boy his parents were believers, hence we feared that he would oppress them rebelliously and ungratefully.' 'Thus we intended for their Lord to exchange in his place one better in purity and nearer in mercifulness.' 'And as for the wall it belonged to two orphan boys within the town. Under it is a treasure belonging to them as their father was a righteous man. So your Lord wanted them to attain the age of adulthood and extract their treasure as a mercy from Him. Therefore I did this not on my own accord. That is the interpretation to which you were impatient.' [Al-Kahf: 71-82]

Sheikh Abdur Rahman ibn Nasir As-Sa'di said:

The story of Khidr as relates to killing the boy and puncturing the boat make evident the second foundation. The circumstance surrounding the killing of the boy, which is an evil/harm, and his overburdening (i.e. oppressively) of his parents along with corrupting their deen, which was a greater evil/harm, eventuated in him perpetrating the least harmful. Furthermore, damaging the boat was an evil/harm; however, seizure of the boat forcibly by the king was a greater evil/harm, so he perpetrated the least of them (in terms of harm).

The issues of jurisprudence and or ijtihaad enter into this from that which is innumerable.[126]

There is no doubt that a person of authority whose ruling is that of disbelief and apostasy—which is the gravest of extremes—or one less than that in magnitude but still deemed as evil, like the extremely oppressive Muslim ruler who usurps the rights of his constituents and openly participates in prohibited acts is a harm, evil, and overt type of corruption. Nonetheless, if attempts to remove him result in the general circumstance of the country becoming worse e.g., the loss of safety and security, the displacing of the average citizens from their homes, the destruction of the peoples' property, the destruction of the country's infrastructure, widespread fighting and killing, the country plunging into instability, and as a result the worship of Allah being halted indefinitely due to the instability; the one bestowed with two eyes by which he sees, two ears by which he hears, and a heart by which he comprehends knows that this circumstance is graver in magnitude than the previously mentioned. Thus the Islamic community must bear patiently with this negative circumstance until Allah bestows relief upon them.

The negative or positive outcomes perceived by actions committed or abandoned was something practiced by the Prophet ﷺ, his Rightly Guided Successors, the remainder of the Companions, and the authorities of knowledge, wisdom, and intelligence among the luminary scholars and specialists of Islamic Sciences that came after them. Therefore assessment of these things is from the prophetic methodology that produces good. The abandonment of this is from the ways of the foolish who produce nothing but turmoil, strife, and misery among the ranks of the Muslims. The following authentic narrations highlight this point:

Aisha, the wife of the Prophet ﷺ, quoted her husband as saying: "Do you not see that your people erected the Kabah but fell short on

---

126. Al-Qawaa'id wal Usool al-Jami'ah.

*building it on the foundation of Ibrahim?" I said, will you not return it
to the foundation of Ibrahim? He replied: "If it wasn't for the fact your
people were recently in disbelief."*[127]

The suggestion of Aisha was good and beneficial; however, the Prophet
صَلَّى ٱللَّهُ عَلَيْهِ وَسَلَّمَ gave precedent to the outcome of that suggestion. He صَلَّى ٱللَّهُ عَلَيْهِ وَسَلَّمَ
perceived that it would be the means to chase them away from Islam on
account of them recently converting from polytheism and still having
unpurged baggage from that experience. So even though the suggestion
was good, he left it due to the negative outcome perceived. Imam An
Nawawi said: "It is evidence to give precedence to the more important
benefit/advantage in the case of infeasibility for all (to come to fruition)."

*Abu Masud al-Ansari said: A man came to Allah's Messenger صَلَّى ٱللَّهُ عَلَيْهِ وَسَلَّمَ
and said "I lag behind on the morning prayer due to so-and-so who
prolongs it." I have never seen the Prophet صَلَّى ٱللَّهُ عَلَيْهِ وَسَلَّمَ more severe
in anger as pertains to an admonition than what I saw that day. He
صَلَّى ٱللَّهُ عَلَيْهِ وَسَلَّمَ said: "O people! Undoubtedly among you are those who chase
people away, thus whoever leads the people—in prayer—then be light
(i.e., don't extend it for long periods) for indeed behind you is the senior
citizen, the weak, and those with a responsibility (i.e., work, etc)."*[128]

Although elongating the standing position in prayer in order to reflect
on what's being recited which causes the heart to soften is beneficial for
those listening, in this circumstance it was a means of causing people to
abandon prayer in congregation due to their varying conditions. This was
something the imam didn't perceive but the Messenger صَلَّى ٱللَّهُ عَلَيْهِ وَسَلَّمَ gave
his instructions to hinder the prayer in congregation from becoming
undesirable. Imam An Nawawi said: "Within it is evidence for being
merciful with those being led in prayer, and to give attention to their
overall wellbeing, along with not causing any difficulty for them."

---

127. Bukhari: 4484 and Muslim: 1333.

128. Bukhari: 704 and Muslim: 467.

Jabir ibn Abdullah said: We were with the Prophet ﷺ during a war expedition when a man from the immigrants shoved a man from the helpers. As a result the man from the helpers summoned the helpers, and the man from the immigrants summoned the immigrants. Consequently Allah's Messenger ﷺ said: "What is this, a call to ignorance?!" They said "O Messenger of Allah a man from the immigrants shoved another from the helpers." He ﷺ replied: "abandon this for indeed it stinks!" Unfortunately Abdullah ibn Ubay heard of the incident and said, "They did this?! I swear by Allah when we return to Medinah the honorable among it will expel these lowly ones." As a result Umar said to the Messenger ﷺ:"Leave me to strike the neck of this hypocrite." He ﷺ replied: "Leave him, lest the people say that Muhammad kills his companions."[129]

The point of reference here is the Prophet's ﷺ keen perception of what would occur if Umar were allowed to assassinate Abdullah ibn Ubay. Although he was from the chief of hypocrites and attempted to sow dissension whenever possible among the ranks of the Muslims, his assassination would have been viewed by those on the outside looking in as negative, consequently turning them away from Islam on account of non Muslims viewing everyone among the Muslims to be of one faith and brotherhood. Imam An Nawawi said while expounding on the benefits derived from the narration: "Patience with some harmful/ corrupt matters due to fear that it could lead to an even greater form of corruption."

THE IMPLICATION OF A JUST WORD TO AN OPPRESSIVE RULER

In contemporary times the relationship between the ruler and his subjects, and the rights he has over them has become muddied. This is due to the peoples' ignorance, from one perspective; and the plots of the disingenuous from another. Regardless which of the two are more responsible—and Allah is All Knower of the reality—both misappropriate

---

129. Muslim: 2584.

the statement of Allah's Messenger ﷺ as pertains to enjoining good upon the oppressive leader:

> *Abu Saeed al-Khudri quoted Allah's Messenger ﷺ as saying: "The best of jihad is a word of justice to the oppressive ruler."*[130]

This authentic narration is commonly cited to justify circulating the faults of a Muslim leader, inciting hatred for him, publicly bashing and insulting him from the pulpit and in other public forums, and whatever is similar to these actions that conflict with the previous authentic narrations with respect to hearing and obeying. Hence in order to debunk the fallacy of such an interpretation it is important to understand how erudite scholars actually view this narration.

Abul Ali Muhammad Abdur Rahman ibn Abdir Raheem al-Mubarakfuri said: "A word of justice" i.e., a word of truth as is reported within a chain of transmission. The intent is that which implies enjoining good and forbidding evil as relates to verbal expression or whatever enters into its meaning like writing (to the ruler), and whatever is similar.[131]

Thus the intent is to speak to the ruler in order to enjoin upon him good and forbid him from committing evil. This in no way entails publicly shaming, bashing, berating, or insulting him nor does it entail the circulation of his sins in order to foster hatred for him or provoke an uprising; on the contrary the intent is advising him with that which will lead him to paradise by discouraging him from committing wrong. The best method in accomplishing this has been encouraged by the Messenger ﷺ in an authentic narration:

> *Iyyad ibn Ghunaym stated that the Prophet ﷺ said: "Whoever desires to advise the ruler do not unexpectedly come in public; instead take him by the hand (i.e., in private) and if he listens then good and if not then he has performed the duty upon him."*[132]

---

130. Abu Dawud: 4344, Tirmidhi: 2174, An-Nisaa'i: 4209 and Ibn Majah: 4011.

131. Tuhfat-ul-Ahwadhi.

132. Kitab-us-Sunnah of ibn Abi Asim | 1096, 1097, 1098.

This is a prophetic directive which is more probable to produce good and benefit for the Muslim community in opposition to acting haphazardly by inciting the community against the leader. This point its substantiation finds more merit when considering Allah's instructions to Musa and Harun as relates to how they should interact with Pharoah. It's equally important to point out that Pharaoh was a pompous infidel who equated himself with Allah. His transgression, oppression, insolence, haughtiness, and recklessness far exceeds the actions of any Muslim in governance or otherwise. Yet Allah issued this directive, He Whose wisdom is perfect and Whose judgment is also perfect:

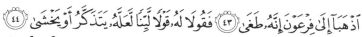

Both of you go to Pharaoh indeed he has transgressed. Speak mildly to him in order for him to accept admonition or fear. [Ta-Ha: 43-44]

Imam Ash-Shawkani said: "Allah ordered them to go to Pharaoh and ordered them with speaking mildly to him due to what is within that of effectiveness/impact as pertains to acceptance."[133]

Thus would we honestly say that contemporary Muslim rulers are worse in status and level than Pharaoh? Would we honestly believe that Allah would prescribe this type of interaction with Pharaoh but prefer a harsher and stricter approach that is more probable to produce chaos with a person who actually acknowledges Allah to be his Lord and has generally submitted to Him by being Muslim? Is Pharaoh better than an oppressive Muslim? The answers to these questions are clear for the person not blinded with ignorance.

Lastly, this was the preferred method of the Companions as it pertains to interacting with the leader in order to produce benefit and to keep the doors of tribulation closed. Within the two authentic collections there is the following:

---

133. Fath-ul-Qadeer.

Ubaydullah ibn al-Khayar said: I came to Usamah ibn Zaid and said to him, "Will you not advise Uthman ibn Affan with respect to establishing the Islamic Legal punishment against Al-Waleed?!" He replied, "Do you think I did not advise him unless it was in your presence?" I swear by Allah I have advised him privately as I don't want to be he who opens the door of evil with me being the first to have done such."

This is wisdom that many in modern times are deprived of, and Allah knows best.

"BUT SOME COMPANIONS REBELLED AGAINST THE RULER"

Amid the arguments utilized by proponents to rebellion against the unjust Muslim ruler is what took place in the annals of history as pertains to a minority among the Companions and the *Tabi'oon*. Although it is true that a minority among them had disputes with certain leaders, their disputes are not deemed proof to legitimize rebellion as we'll see shortly by Allah's permission. Prior to initiation of this particular subject, it is of great importance to understand who is referred to by this doubt.

- Abdullah ibn-uz-Zubayr: He had a dispute with Yazid ibn Muawiyah.
- Husayn ibn Ali ibn Abi Talib: He also had a dispute with Yazid.

When expounding on this affair it is of great importance to comprehend if the statements and actions of the Companions are proof to which others besides them are obliged to follow. Equally important to understand is if a single Companion says or does something is it viewed in the same capacity as the Companions in their entirety. Only with comprehension of these two things can we approach the subject with a clearer path that arrives at the truth in this regard.

First, the consensus of the Companions is evidence in the religion. This is an undeniable reality based on text within the noble book and the purified prophetic traditions. The following text illustrate this important point:

وَمَن يُشَاقِقِ ٱلرَّسُولَ مِنۢ بَعْدِ مَا تَبَيَّنَ لَهُ ٱلْهُدَىٰ وَيَتَّبِعْ غَيْرَ سَبِيلِ ٱلْمُؤْمِنِينَ نُوَلِّهِۦ مَا تَوَلَّىٰ وَنُصْلِهِۦ جَهَنَّمَ ۖ وَسَآءَتْ مَصِيرًا

And whoever contends with the Messenger after the guidance has been made clear to him and follows a path other than that of the believers, We shall keep him on the path he has chosen and will burn him in Hell, an evil destination. [An-Nisa: 115]

Sheikh Muhammad al-Amin Ash-Shinqiti said: Within it is a threat in following other than the believers' path and their path is whatever (subject) they have consensus.[134]

Ibn Hazm al-Andalousi said:

Undoubtedly they—may Allah be pleased with them—were the entirety of the believers as there was no believer among mankind besides them. Interestingly, whoever's characteristic is this, then (his, along with those with him) their consensus is the consensus of the believers.[135]

Sheikh Abdur Rahman ibn Nasir As-Sa'di said: Their path i.e. their way as pertains to their creed and actions.[136]

This is from the clearest of evidence substantiating this point that is often quoted by the people of knowledge to support their argument. The verse refers to the path of the believers i.e. that which they unanimously agreed upon in terms of what Islam is and consists of with regards to creed, worship, code of conduct, business transactions, governance, etc. Whatsoever they unanimously agreed upon and enacted is their path to which the threat of abandonment of it is connected.

فَإِنْ ءَامَنُوا بِمِثْلِ مَآ ءَامَنتُم بِهِۦ فَقَدِ ٱهْتَدَوا ۖ وَّإِن تَوَلَّوْا فَإِنَّمَا هُمْ فِى شِقَاقٍ ۖ فَسَيَكْفِيكَهُمُ ٱللَّهُ ۚ وَهُوَ ٱلسَّمِيعُ ٱلْعَلِيمُ

---

134. Mudhakkir Usool Al-Fiqh.

135. Al-Ihkam.

136. Tayseer Al-Kareem Al-Mannan.

Thus if they believe with equal to what you believe then they are guided; but if they turn away, then they are only in opposition... [Al-Baqara: 137]

Imam Ash-Shawkani said: This address is directed to the Muslims also i.e., if the people of the book and others besides them believe equally to what you believe from all of Allah's books and messengers, and do not divide between anyone among them, at that point they are guided.[137]

This verse is explicit in expressing the obligation of belief identical to that of the Companions. The sentence has a conditional clause making one thing binding in order to achieve another. In layman's terms, guidance cannot be achieved without belief being identical to the belief of the Companions, and there is no doubt that the Companions had unanimous agreement with regards to their creed. In other words, there is no guidance for he whose creed is the polar opposite or stands in stark contrast to the Companions regardless if they be Jew, Christian, Hindu, Buddist, or one who affirms for himself Islam.

وَٱلسَّٰبِقُونَ ٱلْأَوَّلُونَ مِنَ ٱلْمُهَٰجِرِينَ وَٱلْأَنصَارِ وَٱلَّذِينَ ٱتَّبَعُوهُم بِإِحْسَٰنٍ رَّضِيَ ٱللَّهُ عَنْهُمْ وَرَضُوا۟ عَنْهُ وَأَعَدَّ لَهُمْ جَنَّٰتٍ تَجْرِى تَحْتَهَا ٱلْأَنْهَٰرُ خَٰلِدِينَ فِيهَآ أَبَدًا ذَٰلِكَ ٱلْفَوْزُ ٱلْعَظِيمُ

And the foremost to embrace Islam from the immigrants and the helpers, and those who follow them with exactitude; Allah is pleased with them, and they with him. He has prepared for them gardens underneath which rivers flow to abide therein forever. This is the superior success. [At-Taubah: 100]

The point of reference in this verse is the portion "and those who follow them with exactitude" i.e. precisely. Allah informs us about what He prepared for the Companions of rewards and mentions that other than them can obtain this reward as well with the condition that they follow

---

137. Fath-ul-Qadeer.

them precisely. Thus if Allah's pleasure and paradise cannot be obtained except by a divinely prescribed means, then the ruling on this means is obligation and no one from the people of knowledge disputes this.

Sheikh Abdur Rahman ibn Nasir As Sa'di said:

...and those who follow them with exactitude" concerning credal matters, speech, and action. Hence they are free from blame as they have obtained the utmost in commendation and the best of gifts/favors from Allah.[138]

The hadith of Abu Musa al-Ashari in which the Prophet ﷺ said:

The stars are a source of safety for the sky, thus when the stars depart that which is promised for the sky will come. Similarly, I am a source of safety for my Companions, so when I depart that which is promised for them will come to pass. Additionally, my Companions are a source of safety for my nation, thus when they depart, what is promised for my nation will come to pass.[139]

Imam An-Nawawi said:

The meaning of the narration is; as long as the stars remain, likewise the sky will remain. However, when the stars fall and scatter during the resurrection the sky will debilitate causing it to fracture, split apart, and vanish. [140]

This is the sentiment with the remainder of the Messenger's ﷺ similitude including the portion emphasizing the Companions. They are a source of security as pertains to one's path towards Allah. Their understanding and practical application of Islam protects the adherent from deviation and corruption as notably illustrated in the aforementioned verses, in the narration quoted now, and in others similar in meaning. For this reason Imam An Nawawi said, about the portion which mentions the Companions:

---

138. Tayseer Al-Kareem Al-Mannan.

139. Muslim: 2531.

140. Sharh Sahih Muslim.

Its meaning is (a safety) from the emergence of innovation and novel mishaps in the religion, trials therein, the rising of the horn of Shaitan, the Romans or others besides them being victorious over them, the desecration of Medina and Mecca, etc.

The hadith of Umar ibn al-Khattab where the Prophet ﷺ said:

> *I advise you with my Companions, then those that follow them, and then those that follow them. Thereafter, lying will spread so much that a man will swear but will not be requested to do so, and another will give testimony to what he witnessed but will not be requested to do so...*[141]

This unequivocally proves the consensus of the Companions is proof and a yardstick in distinguishing truth from falsehood and guidance from deviance. In contrast to the issue concerning an individual among the Companions, is his statement or action proof? This issue is approached differently and is not viewed in the same manner as its predecessor. The scholars, when approaching this issue, apply guidelines in determining if it constitutes evidence. If the speech or action of a single Companion meets the criteria laid out by the people of knowledge then in this instance it's determined to be evidence. So, what are these guidelines applied by the scholars? They are as follows:

- A Companion's statement doesn't oppose anything reported within neither the Quran nor authentic Sunnah.
- It doesn't oppose the speech of another Companion, if so the one whose speech is closer to the text is whose speech is accepted.
- An individual among the Companions' speech becomes widespread and far reaching, yet all Companions remain quiet about his speech, as this illustrates the lack of objection to the speech and what it entails.

If these components are in place, then the speech is proof; however, if they are not in place, then the speech is not viewed from an evidentiary perspective, and Allah knows best. In light of this it isn't correct to

---

141. Tirmidhi: 2165.

justify rebelling against a Muslim ruler due to sinfulness and oppression on account that it clashes with the Quran and Sunnah as is illustrated throughout this discourse. Hence, the attempt to substantiate such by way of Abdullah ibn Zubayr's actions or that of Husayn ibn Ali's is nothing more than a claim standing in dire need of proof, especially considering the fact that other Companions were not congruent with their decision and Allah knows best.

IS THERE IJMAA ON THE PROHIBITION OF REBELLING AGAINST THE OPPRESSIVE MUSLIM RULER?

Of utmost importance to clarify with respect to the oppressive ruler is that there are differing opinions held with regards to rebellion among the people of knowledge and leading specialists in fiqh jurisprudence. Although there is a declaration of consensus regarding the prohibition of revolting against the oppressive ruler—most notably from Imam An-Nawawi and a multitude of scholars besides him-, the reality is there exist among some scholars a difference of opinion. To illustrate this point further, I'll present some statements of the scholar and specialist in fiqh Muhammad ibn Ibrahim al-Wazeer from his work *Al-Awasim wal Qawasim* (العواصم والقواصم) by Allah's permission:

> Indeed the speech pertaining to rebelling against the tyrannical ruler is a speculative issue with them (i.e. the scholars of fiqh jurisprudence). Thus he who rebels against the oppressive—deeming it to be permissible—is not a sinner, due to him acting according to his independent judgment (based on jurist principles to derive a ruling i.e. ijtihad) with respect to this speculative subsidiary issue. Therefore he does not merit the ruling of sinner, nor is his action described as prohibited by those who view it as permissible. Furthermore, more than one among them as mentioned what makes this necessary, among them is Ar-Raazi in his book *Forty* as pertains to fundamentals of the religion, also his virtuous teacher al-Alawi (i.e. Sulaiman ibn Ibrahim ibn Umar Nafis-ud-Deen al-Alawi at-Tazi al-Yamani).

Muhammad Al-Wazeer also said:

> Al-Qadhi Iyyadh said, 'If there emerges from him (i.e. the leader) disbelief, or alteration of the Islamic Legislation, or innovation then he

is expelled from the ruling of authority and obedience to him is dropped. Likewise it becomes obligatory on the Muslims to stand against him, and install a righteous leader in his place if they are able to do so, even if that does not occur except by way of a small group. Additionally, it is compulsory to stand up by removing a disbeliever; however, it is not compulsory with the innovator unless it is overwhelmingly believed there's ability. If inability is materialized then it is not compulsory. Hence the Muslim migrates from his land to another and flees with his religion.' He also said, 'Some of them said that it is compulsory to remove him unless tribulations result from doing such.' End quote; al-Alawi reports this from him.

Also his statement:

When Abu Abdillah ibn Mujahid (i.e. At-Taaee) alleged consensus on the prohibition of rebelling against the tyrannical ruler, they refuted that and denounced him. Ibn Hazm was among those who refuted him, so how about others besides him? Ibn Hazm uses as proof against him the rebellion of Husayn ibn Ali against Yazid ibn Mu'awiyya and the rebellion of ibn Ash'ath and those with him from the major Tabi'een against Hajjaj, he mentions this in his book *Al-Ijmaa*. Ar-Reemay reports it from him in the last section of a book titled *Al Ijmaa* in the order he assigned for it. So ibn Hazm said: 'I saw from some who attributes himself to a level of knowledge related authority and speech in the religion render judgment and mention therein a consensus. Thus he comes with speech that had he remained silent it would be better from him in the end...'

Additionally he said:

Among those who disapprove of ibn Mujahid's claims of consensus in this issue is Al Qadhi Iyyadh al-Maliki, as he said, 'Some of the scholars refute him with the stance of Husayn ibn Ali and ibn Zubayr, the people of Medinah against Bani Umayya, a large portion of the Tabi'een and the first wave with ibn Ash'ath against Hajjaj. The statement (of the Prophet) 'Also to not contest the authority of he who is in office' was interpreted as not contesting the righteous/just leader.

Furthermore, Al Qadhi Iyyadh said, 'The proof of the majority is that their standing against Hajjaj wasn't strictly due to sinfulness, on the contrary due to what he changed of the legislation and displayed of disbelief.' This is a clarification of their agreement on improvement of (the reasoning behind) what Husayn and his comrades did along with ibn Ash'ath and his comrades. So the majority restrict the allowance of rebellion to whoever's characteristics are like that, while some of them allow rebellion against every tyrant.'

These statements are sufficient in terms of relaying and clarifying this important point. Likewise this commentary is sufficient—and Allah knows best—in clarifying some of the intricacies surrounding this issue and it is hoped that the reader benefits from what was mentioned, and with Allah is success.

The Fourth Principle

Author

The elucidation of knowledge and the scholars, and Islamic jurisprudence and the Islamic Jurists, along with clarifying who resembles them yet is not from them. Allah clarifies this in the beginning portions of surah al baqara, from His statement, "O descendants of Israel! Remember My favor I bestowed upon you and fulfill my covenant and I—in turn—will fulfill—the terms of—your covenant.." until His statement "O descendants of Israel! Remember My favor I bestowed upon you, and indeed I showed you preference over the rest of creation." [Al-Baqara:47-40]

He adds clarity—i.e. to this affair—by what the Sunnah made apparent as relates to clear, abundant, and manifest speech for the unintelligent commoner. Thereafter this became the strangest of things. Knowledge and Islamic Jurisprudence became innovation and misguidance, thus the best of what they possessed was a mixture of truth with falsehood. Consequently, knowledge that Allah made binding upon His creation and praised, no one uttered it except a heretic or one mentally challenged. Moreover whoever disapproved of, and held hostility towards it along with warning against and prohibiting it then he is the jurist and or scholar.

This particular principle pertains to Islamic knowledge and what is connected to it as relates to its meaning, its virtue, its types, its positive effects on the community, etc. This subject is of extreme importance because it makes clear the significance of knowledge and its carrier along with enabling the Muslims to distinguish between actual people of knowledge and those who resemble them but in reality are not from them.

WHAT IS KNOWLEDGE?

In terms of Islamic scholarship, knowledge (*ilm*) is depicted as being comprehension and awareness whose opposite is ignorance. It is also defined as, the perception of things as they are unwaveringly. Additionally; it is said that knowledge is the perception of a thing upon its true reality, or awareness of a thing by way of evidence. The erudite scholar of fiqh and Arabic language Sheikh Muhammad al-Uthaymin said, "It is comprehension of a thing upon what its true reality is, with an unwavering perception." This definition is mentioned while listing the levels of comprehension, the remainder of these levels—from his speech—are as follows:

- Simple Ignorance and it is the lack of comprehending something in totality.
- Compounded Ignorance and it is comprehension of a thing upon a way that opposes its true reality/nature.
- Conjecture (wahm) and it is the comprehension of a thing consisting with the (overwhelming) possibility of being opposite to the probable.
- Doubt and it is the comprehension of a thing (possibly having more than one interpretation or reality) and all probabilities are equal.
- Hypothetical Reasoning and it is comprehension of a matter that's coupled with being opposite to the least probable (in terms of its true reality).

These levels are of the utmost importance when acquiring understanding of *Qawa'idul Fiqh* and its practical application when applied to actual situations that arise within Muslim communities, insomuch that they are pivotal when assessing and placing a ruling on something or someone or refraining from such due to something obstructing the ruling's validity. In layman's terms, these levels of comprehension, when understood and applied properly, could be the distinguishing factor in a ruling being valid or void. For clarification purposes, let's look at the types of ignorance mentioned previously and look at how they may affect a ruling's validity.

> *Abu Dharr al-Ghifari narrated the speech of the Messenger ﷺ as:* *"Undoubtedly Allah has overlooked for my nation errors, forgetfulness, and when forced to do something."*

Among the things overlooked is when a Muslim makes a mistake. Most mistakes emanate from a lack of knowledge, regardless if the ignorance is simple or compounded. So if a person does an act or falls short in implementation of an act based on ignorance, then he is not deemed sinful with Allah and the sin normally applied is overlooked. As an illustration we have the following authentic narration of Adi ibn Hatim and it is as follows:

> When the verse was revealed **"until the white thread is distinguished from the black thread of the dawn"** [Al Baqarah: 187]. Adi ibn Hatim said: "O Messenger of Allah! I have placed under my pillow two threads/cords. One white and one black in order to determine the night from the day." Allah's Messenger ﷺ replied: "Your pillow must be very expansive as it (i.e. the verses intent) is strictly the black of night and the white of day."[142]

Imam An Nawawi said:

> Although the meaning of the narration has many explanations, the best (and more correct) is the speech of Al Qadhi Iyyadh—may Allah have mercy on him—when he said, "He only acquired the two threads and placed them under his head interpreting the verse because his

---

142. Muslim: 1090 and Bukhari: 1917.

initial understanding was that this was intended. Likewise others besides him did the same until the revealing of the portion 'from the dawn' as a result they understood it to be the whiteness of the day and darkness of night."[143]

Thus several important points are extracted from this narration and they are as follows:

- He wasn't commanded to repeat the fast for those days.
- He wasn't deemed sinful.
- He was neither chastised nor reprimanded.
- His understanding came from the text itself.
- He was deliberate in trying to please Allah and not evade the obligation of fasting.

It is clear that Adi ibn Hatim had with him compounded ignorance in this instance. He understood the text in an improper manner and acted on that improper understanding. Despite his actions overtly being in conflict with the fast, no ruling can be placed on him as sinful in this regard due to his misinterpretation of the text being that which obstructs the validity of such a ruling. Comparatively this condition is assessed in matters of *takfir* (judging a Muslim to be an apostate), and *tabdi* (judging a Sunni to be an innovator) and can be the determining factor as pertains to the ruling being valid or not.

Additionally, assessment of the other types of comprehension also indicate their significance in judging a situation properly. To clarify, we have the level rendered into English as conjecture (*wahm*); which is a statement or situation having two possible meanings with the less probable being deemed conjecture (*wahm*). In other words it is a possibility that is far from being accurate or plausible. This is the intent of the powerful Islamic principle "There's no reliance in conjecture (*wahm*)" i.e. there's no reliance on that which has no evidence to support it as it is highly improbable, so no action is initiated or postponed on account of it and no ruling results from it.

---

143. Sharh Sahih Muslim.

Sheikh Salih As-Sadlan said concerning this principle: "Undoubtedly conjecture is false. No ruling is built upon it, no judgment is prevented by it, no right is postponed on account of it. In other words, no Islamic ruling is established with it, just as no Islamic ruling is delayed on account of it." The Sheikh also said:

> However, conjecture (*wahm*) there is no consideration given towards it nor is there any reliance upon it with respect to all subjects of jurisprudence from worship, transactions, judgment, testimony, crimes, rights, etc. This is the best evidence for the just nature of the Islamic Legislation insomuch that there is no room for delusional presumption and no reliance upon doubt and desires. None of these things benefits the truth nor stands in its place in any way; only clear certainty and manifest truth investigated with precision and being concerned with the rights (of the people).[144]

This is sufficient in illustrating the importance of understanding these levels of comprehension and how they play a role in affecting the outcome to a judgment in Islam, and Allah knows best.

THE CATEGORIES OF KNOWLEDGE

As pertains to the categories of knowledge, they essentially are divided into two parent categories; beneficial knowledge and non beneficial knowledge. Each category has subdivisions that clarify its importance or its detriment. Ibn Rajab said: "Surely at times Allah The Exalted mentioned knowledge in His book from the angle of praise and it is beneficial knowledge, and other times He mentions it from the perspective of blame and it is knowledge that is not beneficial."[145]

So the first category, beneficial knowledge is any knowledge that is favorable for the one who acquires it and this category has two subdivisions. They are as follows:

- World Related Knowledge: it is knowledge that benefits its possessor in this worldly life, e.g. mathematics, reading,

---

144. Al-Qawaaid Al-Fiqhiyyah Al-Kubra.

145. Fadl Ilm As-Salaf.

engineering, medicine, carpentry, computer programming, etc.
- Islamic Legislative Knowledge: it is knowledge that benefits its possessor in this life and in the Hereafter on account of it clarifying the path which leads to paradise.

Islamic Legislative Knowledge is what's intended within the Quran and Sunnah when knowledge is praised. Not only is this knowledge praised but likewise its possessor and its seeker. The following are some of the textual evidences alluding to this.

وَمِنَ ٱلنَّاسِ وَٱلدَّوَآبِّ وَٱلْأَنْعَٰمِ مُخْتَلِفٌ أَلْوَٰنُهُۥ كَذَٰلِكَ إِنَّمَا يَخْشَى ٱللَّهَ مِنْ عِبَادِهِ ٱلْعُلَمَٰٓؤُا۟ إِنَّ ٱللَّهَ عَزِيزٌ غَفُورٌ

The possessors of knowledge are the only ones that fear Allah among His servants... [Fatir: 28]

قُلْ هَلْ يَسْتَوِى ٱلَّذِينَ يَعْلَمُونَ وَٱلَّذِينَ لَا يَعْلَمُونَ إِنَّمَا يَتَذَكَّرُ أُو۟لُوا۟ ٱلْأَلْبَٰبِ

Say: Are those that know equal to those that don't know? Only the possessors of knowledge will remember. [Az-Zumar: 9]

وَتِلْكَ ٱلْأَمْثَٰلُ نَضْرِبُهَا لِلنَّاسِ وَمَا يَعْقِلُهَآ إِلَّا ٱلْعَٰلِمُونَ

And these are the parables We put forth to mankind, and no one comprehends them except the possessors of knowledge. [Al-Ankabut: 43]

يَرْفَعِ ٱللَّهُ ٱلَّذِينَ ءَامَنُوا۟ مِنكُمْ وَٱلَّذِينَ أُوتُوا۟ ٱلْعِلْمَ دَرَجَٰتٍ وَٱللَّهُ بِمَا تَعْمَلُونَ خَبِيرٌ

Allah raises those who believe among you and those who have been given knowledge in ranks, and Allah is Well Acquainted with what you do. [Al-Mujadilah: 11]

شَهِدَ ٱللَّهُ أَنَّهُۥ لَآ إِلَٰهَ إِلَّا هُوَ وَٱلْمَلَٰٓئِكَةُ وَأُو۟لُوا۟ ٱلْعِلْمِ

Allah, the angels, and the possessors of knowledge bear witness that there is no deity in truth except Him... [Ali-Imran: 18]

وَمَا كَانَ ٱلْمُؤْمِنُونَ لِيَنفِرُوا۟ كَآفَّةً فَلَوْلَا نَفَرَ مِن كُلِّ فِرْقَةٍ مِّنْهُمْ طَآئِفَةٌ لِّيَتَفَقَّهُوا۟ فِى ٱلدِّينِ وَلِيُنذِرُوا۟ قَوْمَهُمْ إِذَا رَجَعُوٓا۟ إِلَيْهِمْ لَعَلَّهُمْ يَحْذَرُونَ

And it is not correct for all of the believers to go out and fight. Only a party from each group should proceed, in order for a group to acquire comprehension of the religion and to warn their people after returning to them in order for them to be cautious (from evil). [Taubah: 122]

قُلْ هَٰذِهِۦ سَبِيلِىٓ أَدْعُوٓا۟ إِلَى ٱللَّهِ عَلَىٰ بَصِيرَةٍ أَنَا۠ وَمَنِ ٱتَّبَعَنِى

Say: This is my path, I invite to Allah upon clear knowledge, me and those that follow me... [Yusuf: 108]

Additionally, within the narrations authentically attributed to the Messenger ﷺ we find further emphasis on the status of Islamic Legislative Knowledge and its virtue. The following are some of these authentic narrations:

> The Prophet's ﷺ statement narrated on the authority of Muawiya ibn Abi Sufyan: "Whoever Allah wants good for He blesses with comprehension of the religion. I am only a distributor; however, Allah is the one Who gives. The affair of this nation will not cease to be straight until the Hour is established or until the command of Allah comes."[146]

Al Hafidh ibn Hajr al-Asqalaani said:

> The intent of the narration is that whoever does not attain comprehension of the religion, i.e. learn Islamic principles and what is connected to it from the subsidiary affairs, has been deprived of good. Abu Ya'la published the narration of Muawiya from another transmission (which is weak) that has the following addition at the end 'Whoever doesn't attain comprehension of the religion Allah is not concerned with him.' This meaning is sound on account that whoever doesn't know the affairs of his religion is neither a faqih nor a seeker of understanding. Thus it is correct to describe him as one who good is not intended for. Included within the narration is a clear clarification for

---

146. Bukhar: 7312 and 71; Muslim: 1037.

the virtue of the scholar over the remainder of men, and the virtue of seeking comprehension of the religion over the remainder of sciences.[147]

The Prophet's ﷺ statement narrated on the authority of Abu Hurairah: "Undoubtedly this world is cursed. That which is within it is cursed except the remembrance of Allah, obedience to Him, and the scholar or seeker of knowledge."[148]

Abul Ali Muhammad Abdur Rahman al-Mubarakfuri said:

The world is cursed because it deceives the soul with its beauty and allure consequently diverting it away from servitude towards desires. Moreover he (i.e. Imam al-Manaawi) said after mentioning his speech about the scholar or seeker of knowledge, 'i.e. it and whatever is in it is distant from Allah except beneficial knowledge that points to Allah, this is the intent.'[149]

The Prophet's ﷺ statement narrated on the authority of Abu Hurairah: "Whoever comes to this masjid of mine and he does not come except for a good to either learn or teach, then he is on the status of the mujahid who goes out on the path of Allah. In contrast to whoever comes for other than that, as he is on the status of a man that looks towards another provision."[150]

Abul Hasan as-Sindi said:

The perspective of resembling the seeker of knowledge with the mujahid upon the path of Allah is on account of enlivening the religion, debasement of the devil, inconveniencing the self and demolishing the shelter of self indulgence. So, how (is it not the case) when it is made permissible for him to fail to participate in jihad?![151]

---

147. Fath-ul-Bari.

148. Tirmidhi: 2322.

149. Tuhfat-ul-Ahwadhi.

150. Ibn Majah: 227.

151. Kifayat-ul-Hajah.

The Prophet's ﷺ *statement narrated on the authority of Abdullah ibn Masud: "There is no envy except in two individuals. A man who Allah has given wealth thus he spends it in accordance with the truth (i.e. obedience to Allah). And a man who Allah has given wisdom, thus he judges by it and teaches it."* [152]

Imam An Nawawi said:

The scholars state that envy has two categories, literal and figurative. As for the literal category it is to desire the removal of a favor from its possessor, and this is forbidden by consensus of this nation along with the authentic text. As for the figurative category it is admiration and that is to desire the exact favor bestowed upon another without it being removed from its possessor. If this is connected to a worldly matter then it is permissible; however, if it is connected to obedience then it is recommended. Additionally, the meaning of the narration is that there is no beloved admiration except for these two things and whatsoever is included within its meaning.[153]

The Prophet's ﷺ *statement narrated on the authority of Abu Darda: "Whoever enters a path desiring, by way of it, knowledge; Allah will enter him (on account of it) on a path that eventuates towards Paradise. Certainly the angels lower their wings being pleased with the seeker of knowledge. Indeed the scholar, everyone within the heavens and the earth even the fish in the oceans seek forgiveness for him. Moreover, the virtues of the scholar over the worshiper is like the virtue of the moon over the remainder of stars. Surely the scholars are the inheritors of the prophets, and the prophets did not leave behind as an inheritance neither gold nor silver; on the contrary they left behind as an inheritance knowledge. Therefore whoever obtains a portion of it, has obtained a plentiful share."*[154]

This narration is self explanatory with respect to its elucidation of the virtues of knowledge, the seeker of knowledge, and the possessor of knowledge.

---

152. Bukhari: 5025 and 7529; Muslim: 816. Translated from his collected verbal expression.

153. Sharh Sahih Muslim.

154. Tirmidhi: 2682.

The Prophet's ﷺ *statement narrated on the authority of Abu Hurairah:* "Whoever relieves a believer from a distress from the troubles of the world, Allah will relieve from him a distress from the troubles of the day of resurrection. Whoever brings ease to a person in straightened conditions, Allah will bring ease to him in this worldly life and in the Hereafter. Whoever covers the fault of a Muslim, Allah will cover his faults in this worldly life and in the Hereafter. Allah is, as relates to aiding his servant; what the servant is, as relates to aiding his brother. Whoever enters a path seeking by way of it knowledge, Allah will make easy for him a path towards Paradise. In addition, no group of people assemble within a house from the houses of Allah (i.e. the masjid) reciting the book of Allah and teaching it to each others, except that tranquility descends upon them, mercy envelopes them, angels surround them, and Allah mentions them to those with Him. So whoever is slowed down by way of his actions, cannot be sped up by way of his lineage."[155]

Ibn Rajab said:

And what is also intended is that Allah facilitates for the seeker of knowledge, when he intends by way of his request the face of Allah The Exalted, benefits from it, and acts accordingly, then it is a means to his guidance and entrance into paradise on account of that. Moreover, He facilitates for the seeker of knowledge other sciences that he benefits from that all are a conduit leading to paradise." He also said, "What is also included within it is the facilitation of (crossing) the best path of paradise on the Day of Resurrection and it is the Sirat and whatsoever is prior to and after it of frightening events that will be made easy.[156]

The Prophet's ﷺ *statement narrated on the authority of Abu Musa al-Ashari:* "The similitude of that which Allah sent me with, of guidance and knowledge, is like an abundance of rain that falls onto land. Among it (the types of land) is that which is pure (i.e. fertile) that accepts the water resulting in pasture and herbage to grow abundantly. Among the types of land is that which is solid/hard and it holds the water. Consequently Allah causes the people to benefit from it. They drink from it, give to their animals to drink, and water vegetation using it. But there is yet another type (i.e. of land) that is flat/even (and barren). It neither holds water nor causes vegetation to grow. This is the similitude of he

---

155. Muslim: 2699.

156. Jami-ul-Uloom wal Hikam.

who comprehends Allah's religion, he is benefitted by what Allah has sent me with, thus he knows and teaches. Furthermore it is a similitude of he who doesn't raise his head towards that (i.e. is unconcerned), and does not accept Allah's guidance that which he sent me with."[157]

Sheikh Ibrahim ibn Sheikh Salih ibn Ahmad al-Khuraisi said:

This narration is tremendous and has major significance. It's inclusive of the categories of man as they are divided into three classifications. The first two are praiseworthy with one of the two being more virtuous than the other. However, the third is blameworthy. So the first depicts whoever accepts the truth, acts accordingly, and teaches it to others. They are the people of memorization and comprehension.

The second classification depicts whoever has a portion committed to memory along with implementation without full comprehension. They are the people of memorization. Consequently Allah benefits the people by way of them and their conveyance of knowledge. This is not accompanied with the derivation of rulings and extraction of its treasures and or benefits.

Lastly, the third are those who are not memorizers, sound interpreters, nor enacters. They are like cattle, on the contrary more astray in terms of their path.[158]

This is sufficient in illustrating the importance of Islamic Legislative Knowledge, its virtue, and why it's praised within the text. As for the second category, non beneficial knowledge, it has two subdivisions as well. They are as follows:

- Neglected Knowledge: The lack of enacting knowledge.
- Blameworthy and Harmful Knowledge: It is knowledge that is of direct detriment to the person who learns it.

Ibn Rajab al-Hanbali said concerning the first type:

Surely He (i.e. Allah) has informed us about a people who were given knowledge, but did not benefit from it. In its essence it is beneficial knowledge; however, its possessor did not benefit from it, The Exalted said (what is rendered into English): **'The similitude of those given**

---

157. Bukhari: 79.

158. Tanbihat Al-Mukhtasirah.

the Torah, but subsequently failed it (i.e. in implementation) is like the donkey that carries a huge burden of books...' [Al-Jumu'ah: 5]

Moreover His statement: '**And recite to them the report of he to whom We gave our signs (i.e. knowledge of revelation), but he threw it away; thus the Shaitan pursued him and he became from those who went astray. And had We willed We surely would have elevated him therewith; however, he clung to the earth and followed his (fruitless) desires...**' [Al-A'raf: 175-176]

Likewise His speech: '**Thereafter a generation succeeded them who inherited the book; however, they chose the obtainment of the goods of this lowly life while saying: "Everything for us will be forgiven." And if the offer was presented (again), they (most certainly) would seize it (i.e. ignoring the guidance).**' [Al-A'raf: 169]

Furthermore His speech: '**And Allah left him to go astray upon knowledge.**' [Al-Jathiyah: 23]

And this is upon the interpretation of those who interpret the verse to mean upon knowledge possessed by he who Allah left astray.[159]

Allah puts forth, as a lesson to humanity within the last revelation, the example of the Jews who exemplified this trait in unambiguous terms. Regardless of the reason behind their actions, whether it be from heedlessness, personal agendas, sinful love of this worldly life, beautification of their vain deeds, or all the above; they are without a shadow of doubt a people who did not enact their knowledge. The following are some verses illustrating this point:

وَإِذْ أَخَذْنَا مِيثَـٰقَكُمْ لَا تَسْفِكُونَ دِمَآءَكُمْ وَلَا تُخْرِجُونَ أَنفُسَكُم مِّن دِيَـٰرِكُمْ ثُمَّ أَقْرَرْتُمْ وَأَنتُمْ تَشْهَدُونَ ﴿٨٤﴾ ثُمَّ أَنتُمْ هَـٰٓؤُلَآءِ تَقْتُلُونَ أَنفُسَكُمْ وَتُخْرِجُونَ فَرِيقًا مِّنكُم مِّن دِيَـٰرِهِمْ تَظَـٰهَرُونَ عَلَيْهِم بِٱلْإِثْمِ وَٱلْعُدْوَٰنِ وَإِن يَأْتُوكُمْ أُسَـٰرَىٰ تُفَـٰدُوهُمْ وَهُوَ مُحَرَّمٌ عَلَيْكُمْ إِخْرَاجُهُمْ ۚ أَفَتُؤْمِنُونَ بِبَعْضِ ٱلْكِتَـٰبِ وَتَكْفُرُونَ بِبَعْضٍ ۚ فَمَا جَزَآءُ مَن يَفْعَلُ ذَٰلِكَ مِنكُمْ إِلَّا خِزْىٌ فِى ٱلْحَيَوٰةِ

---

159. Fadl Ilm As-Salaf.

ٱلدُّنْيَا ۖ وَيَوْمَ ٱلْقِيَٰمَةِ يُرَدُّونَ إِلَىٰ أَشَدِّ ٱلْعَذَابِ ۗ وَمَا ٱللَّهُ بِغَٰفِلٍ عَمَّا تَعْمَلُونَ ﴿٨٥﴾

And when We made binding your covenant that you will neither spill blood nor expel your people from their dwellings. Thereafter you endorsed it and bore witness (to it). Subsequent to that, you killed yourselves, expelled a group of you from their homes, and gave support against them in sin and transgression. But if they come to you as captives you ransom them, although it was (initially) forbidden for you their expulsion. So do you believe in a portion of the book and disbelieve in a portion? Thus what is the recompense of those who do such among you except humiliation in this worldly life, and on the day of resurrection you will be returned to a severe punishment, and Allah is not heedless of what you do. [Al-Baqarah: 84-85]

ٱلَّذِينَ ءَاتَيْنَٰهُمُ ٱلْكِتَٰبَ يَعْرِفُونَهُۥ كَمَا يَعْرِفُونَ أَبْنَاءَهُمْ ۖ وَإِنَّ فَرِيقًا مِّنْهُمْ لَيَكْتُمُونَ ٱلْحَقَّ وَهُمْ يَعْلَمُونَ

Those who We gave the scripture have knowledge of him just as they have knowledge of their own sons. However, a faction among them surely conceals the truth while they know. [Al-Baqarah: 146]

يَٰبَنِىٓ إِسْرَٰٓءِيلَ ٱذْكُرُوا۟ نِعْمَتِىَ ٱلَّتِىٓ أَنْعَمْتُ عَلَيْكُمْ وَأَوْفُوا۟ بِعَهْدِىٓ أُوفِ بِعَهْدِكُمْ وَإِيَّٰىَ فَٱرْهَبُونِ ﴿٤٠﴾ ...

وَلَا تَلْبِسُوا۟ ٱلْحَقَّ بِٱلْبَٰطِلِ وَتَكْتُمُوا۟ ٱلْحَقَّ وَأَنتُمْ تَعْلَمُونَ ﴿٤٢﴾ وَأَقِيمُوا۟ ٱلصَّلَوٰةَ وَءَاتُوا۟ ٱلزَّكَوٰةَ وَٱرْكَعُوا۟ مَعَ ٱلرَّٰكِعِينَ ﴿٤٣﴾ أَتَأْمُرُونَ ٱلنَّاسَ بِٱلْبِرِّ وَتَنسَوْنَ أَنفُسَكُمْ وَأَنتُمْ تَتْلُونَ ٱلْكِتَٰبَ أَفَلَا تَعْقِلُونَ ﴿٤٤﴾

O descendants of Israel! Remember My favor that I bestowed upon you, and fulfill My Covenant so that I will fulfill your covenant (with Me), and fear none but Me... And do not cover the truth with falsehood and conceal the truth while you know. And perform the prayer, give the annual charity, and bow with those who bow. Do you order the people to implement good, but forget to impose it on yourselves while you read the book?! Have you no sense?! [Al-Baqarah: 40 and 42-44]

The second subdivision, Blameworthy and or Harmful Knowledge is best explained by Allah's statement in Al Baqarah verse 102:

وَٱتَّبَعُواْ مَا تَتْلُواْ ٱلشَّيَـٰطِينُ عَلَىٰ مُلْكِ سُلَيْمَـٰنَ وَمَا كَفَرَ سُلَيْمَـٰنُ وَلَـٰكِنَّ ٱلشَّيَـٰطِينَ كَفَرُواْ يُعَلِّمُونَ ٱلنَّاسَ ٱلسِّحْرَ وَمَآ أُنزِلَ عَلَى ٱلْمَلَكَيْنِ بِبَابِلَ هَـٰرُوتَ وَمَـٰرُوتَ وَمَا يُعَلِّمَانِ مِنْ أَحَدٍ حَتَّىٰ يَقُولَآ إِنَّمَا نَحْنُ فِتْنَةٌ فَلَا تَكْفُرْ فَيَتَعَلَّمُونَ مِنْهُمَا مَا يُفَرِّقُونَ بِهِۦ بَيْنَ ٱلْمَرْءِ وَزَوْجِهِۦ وَمَا هُم بِضَآرِّينَ بِهِۦ مِنْ أَحَدٍ إِلَّا بِإِذْنِ ٱللَّهِ وَيَتَعَلَّمُونَ مَا يَضُرُّهُمْ وَلَا يَنفَعُهُمْ وَلَقَدْ عَلِمُواْ لَمَنِ ٱشْتَرَىٰهُ مَا لَهُۥ فِى ٱلْءَاخِرَةِ مِنْ خَلَـٰقٍ وَلَبِئْسَ مَا شَرَوْاْ بِهِۦٓ أَنفُسَهُمْ لَوْ كَانُواْ يَعْلَمُونَ

And they followed what the devils distributed (by word of mouth through lessons, and their writings) during the reign of Sulaiman. Sulaiman did not disbelieve; however, the devils disbelieved by teaching the people magic (sihr) and that which came down to the two angels Harut and Marut at Babylon. None of the two (angels) taught anyone (anything) except that they said (beforehand), "Undoubtedly we are but a trial so do not disbelieve!" Consequently they learned from the two that which causes a split between husband and wife; however, they weren't a harm to anyone except with the permission of Allah. They (the people) learned that which harmed them and did not benefit them. Certainly they knew that the buyers of it would have no portion (of good) in the Hereafter, and bad was that for which they sold themselves if they only knew.

There are several statements within this verse that indicate the extremely harmful nature of acquiring this knowledge, thus making it blameworthy in the Islamic sense. They are as follows:

- "They followed what the devils distributed"
- "The devils disbelieved by teaching the people magic"
- "Undoubtedly we are but a trial so do not disbelieve"
- "They (the people) learned that which harmed them and did not benefit them"
- "The buyers of it would have no portion (of good) in the Hereafter"
- "And bad was that for which they sold themselves"

This points to the detriment of teaching, learning, and enactment of magic (*sihr*) in unambiguous terms. In other words, the ruling on teaching, learning, and enactment of magic is undeniably clear, that being prohibition. But what is magic? The scholars have elucidated its Islamic technical definition. The following are some of their statements:

Sheikh Salih Alish-Sheikh said:

> As for magic that is deemed disbelief and major polytheism with Allah it is usage of devils and seeking their assistance in order to achieve a matter, by a means of nearness to that devil with an act from the varying acts of worship. Moreover, magic has been defined by the scholars of Fiqh Jurisprudence as spells, incantations, and knots blown into; resulting in magic literally harming, sickening, and killing (its victim).[160]

Sheikh Salih al-Fawzan said:

> An expression applied to action that affects the body or the heart. It affects the body by sickening or killing it. Likewise it affects the thoughts by influencing a person to believe he did an act that he did not do. Also it affects the heart, by way of it (magic) hatred is fostered, or love that is unnatural. This is what is referred to as *Sarf* (manufacturing an aversion) and *Atif* (influencing an inclination towards something) to the extent that a person is made to have a favorable disposition that produces within him love that is unnatural for something or someone; or causes hatred for that thing similar to how it causes separation

---

160. At-Tamheed the Explanation of Kitab At Tawheed.

between a husband and wife.[161]

Sheikh Ibrahim ibn Sheikh Salih ibn Ahmad al-Khuraisi said: "Knots and incantations used by the magician as a means to employ the devils to harm the one bewitched. Additionally, it is said its definition is other than that due to the differing of its types."[162]

Thus magic (*sihr*) is any ritual incantation or spell, or any speech spoken or written, or any act performed that consequently affects the heart, body, or mind in an adverse manner which causes impairment or death or affects the emotions causing an inclining towards something or aversion for it, and Allah knows best. Of notable importance is the fact that magic is classified as having two categories. The first category is actual magic and its definition is what was previously mentioned from the statements of the scholars. The second category is imaginative or deceptive magic; i.e. that which is done with usage of smoke and mirrors, or sleights of the hand, or some other deceptive means which confuses one's perception leading one to believe something is what it is not. Similar to what is witnessed at magic shows within circuses.

Sheikh Muhammad Al-Imam said:

Not every magician is an ally with the devils of the jinn, on the contrary there are some magicians practicing magic yet their magic is from the perspective of trickery and deceit. Nonetheless, they do not escape the judgment of being magicians and although the ruling upon them is from the perspective of their level religiously, they do not exit from Islam towards disbelief by way of their actions. However, they are committers of criminality and the excessively grave of sins.[163]

In the encyclopedia of aqeedah, religions, sects, and contemporary doctrines it is stated:

The category of imaginative or deception related magic, is magic that causes a person to perceive something that actually did not occur, similar to the magic of Pharaoh's magicians. The Exalted says:

---

161. Sharh Nawaqid-ul-Islam.

162. Tanbihat Al-Mukhtasirah.

163. Irshad An-Nathir.

'It appeared to him (i.e. Musa) on account of their magic that they moved.' [Ta-Ha: 66]

Thus their magic there is nothing more to it except forms of trickery that frighten due to its outward appearance, which consequently affects the heart.[164]

The following are some of the verses concerning this event between Musa and the magicians of Pharaoh:

وَقَالَ مُوسَىٰ يَٰفِرْعَوْنُ إِنِّى رَسُولٌ مِّن رَّبِّ ٱلْعَٰلَمِينَ ۝ حَقِيقٌ عَلَىٰ أَن لَّآ أَقُولَ عَلَى ٱللَّهِ إِلَّا ٱلْحَقَّ قَدْ جِئْتُكُم بِبَيِّنَةٍ مِّن رَّبِّكُمْ فَأَرْسِلْ مَعِىَ بَنِىٓ إِسْرَٰٓءِيلَ ۝ قَالَ إِن كُنتَ جِئْتَ بِـَٔايَةٍ فَأْتِ بِهَآ إِن كُنتَ مِنَ ٱلصَّٰدِقِينَ ۝ فَأَلْقَىٰ عَصَاهُ فَإِذَا هِىَ ثُعْبَانٌ مُّبِينٌ ۝ وَنَزَعَ يَدَهُ فَإِذَا هِىَ بَيْضَآءُ لِلنَّٰظِرِينَ ۝ قَالَ ٱلْمَلَأُ مِن قَوْمِ فِرْعَوْنَ إِنَّ هَٰذَا لَسَٰحِرٌ عَلِيمٌ ۝ يُرِيدُ أَن يُخْرِجَكُم مِّنْ أَرْضِكُمْ فَمَاذَا تَأْمُرُونَ ۝ قَالُوٓا أَرْجِهْ وَأَخَاهُ وَأَرْسِلْ فِى ٱلْمَدَآئِنِ حَٰشِرِينَ ۝ يَأْتُوكَ بِكُلِّ سَٰحِرٍ عَلِيمٍ ۝ وَجَآءَ ٱلسَّحَرَةُ فِرْعَوْنَ قَالُوٓا إِنَّ لَنَا لَأَجْرًا إِن كُنَّا نَحْنُ ٱلْغَٰلِبِينَ ۝ قَالَ نَعَمْ وَإِنَّكُمْ لَمِنَ ٱلْمُقَرَّبِينَ ۝ قَالُوا يَٰمُوسَىٰٓ إِمَّآ أَن تُلْقِىَ وَإِمَّآ أَن نَّكُونَ نَحْنُ ٱلْمُلْقِينَ ۝ قَالَ أَلْقُوا فَلَمَّآ أَلْقَوْا سَحَرُوٓا أَعْيُنَ ٱلنَّاسِ وَٱسْتَرْهَبُوهُمْ وَجَآءُو بِسِحْرٍ عَظِيمٍ ۝ وَأَوْحَيْنَآ إِلَىٰ مُوسَىٰٓ أَنْ أَلْقِ عَصَاكَ فَإِذَا هِىَ تَلْقَفُ مَا يَأْفِكُونَ ۝

And Musa said, 'O Pharaoh! Surely I am a messenger from the Lord of all existence. 'Correct for me is that I do not say anything about Allah except the truth. Undoubtedly I have come to you with clear proof from your Lord, so send the Descendants of Israel with me.'

---

164. Volume 3.

He replied, 'If you have come with a sign then bring it forth, if you are among the truthful.' Then he (Musa) threw his stick and it (became) an apparent snake. And he removed his hand and it was white (with radiance, glow) for all that see. The chiefs of Pharaoh said, 'Undoubtedly this is a knowledgeable magician.' 'He wants to expel you from your land, so what is your command?' They said, 'Delay him and his brother (for a period), and send recruiters to the cities.' 'They will come to you with every knowledgeable magician.' So Pharaoh's magicians came and they said, 'There will be a great reward for us if we are the winners.' He (Pharaoh) said, 'yes, and you will also be among those brought near.' They said, 'O Musa! Either you throw (first), or we shall throw.' He (Musa) replied, 'Throw!' Hence when they threw they bewitched the eyes of the people and frightened them. They came with great (i.e. convincing) magic. And We revealed to Musa, 'Throw your stick!' It then swallowed up the falsehood they displayed. [Al-A'raf: 104-117]

قَالُوا۟ يَٰمُوسَىٰٓ إِمَّآ أَن تُلْقِىَ وَإِمَّآ أَن نَّكُونَ أَوَّلَ مَنْ أَلْقَىٰ ﴿٦٥﴾ قَالَ بَلْ أَلْقُوا۟ فَإِذَا حِبَالُهُمْ وَعِصِيُّهُمْ يُخَيَّلُ إِلَيْهِ مِن سِحْرِهِمْ أَنَّهَا تَسْعَىٰ ﴿٦٦﴾ فَأَوْجَسَ فِى نَفْسِهِۦ خِيفَةً مُّوسَىٰ ﴿٦٧﴾ قُلْنَا لَا تَخَفْ إِنَّكَ أَنتَ ٱلْأَعْلَىٰ ﴿٦٨﴾ وَأَلْقِ مَا فِى يَمِينِكَ تَلْقَفْ مَا صَنَعُوٓا۟ إِنَّمَا صَنَعُوا۟ كَيْدُ سَٰحِرٍ وَلَا يُفْلِحُ ٱلسَّاحِرُ حَيْثُ أَتَىٰ ﴿٦٩﴾

They said, 'O Musa! Either you throw or we will be the first to throw.' He replied, 'You throw!' Behold their ropes and sticks, it appeared to him (i.e. Musa) on account of their magic that they moved. Thus Musa harbored within himself fear. We said (i.e. to Musa), 'Fear not! Certainly you will be the victor.' 'And throw what is in your right hand, it will swallow what they produced. That which they manufactured is only a magician's craftiness, and the magician will never be successful however he comes.' [Ta-Ha: 65-69]

This category of magic is prohibited as well, and the least that can be said about a person who indulges in such is that he is a highly skilled artist of deception, fraud, and trickery all of which are shunned in the religion and are characteristics not befitting for someone who believes in Allah and the Last Day to adopt. Sheikh-ul-Islam ibn Taymiyyah said: "Magic is forbidden by the Book, Sunnah, and *Ijmaa* (i.e. consensus)."[165] Thus no category is permitted; however, one category is worse than the other. Literal Magic is worse than Deceptive Magic because it cannot be except with obedience to the devils among the Jinn, and whatever else they require—from acts of disbelief—in order to solicit their assistance. Therefore the magician in reality is a polytheist on account of servitude, that which is due to Allah alone, being directed to the devils among the Jinn in exchange for their assistance, and Allah knows best.

Of importance to emphasize, Harmful Knowledge is not restricted to magic, on the contrary magic was mentioned to illustrate clearly how learning some things can be detrimental to one's well being in this life and in the Hereafter. It was not meant to be exclusive to it alone, rather any knowledge regardless of what it may be, if it causes harm to its possessor then it falls into this category and Allah knows best.

THE RULING ON SEEKING KNOWLEDGE

We have seen previously that Islamic Legislative Knowledge is praiseworthy to learn as it is what Sheikh Muhammad ibn Abdul Wahhab stated as being: "Knowledge of Allah, His Prophet, and awareness of the religion of Islam by its evidence." So what is the ruling as relates to acquiring it? The answer to this relevant question is found in the statement of Allah's Messenger ﷺ and it is as follows: "Seeking knowledge is obligatory upon every Muslim."[166]

Imam As-Suyuti expounds on this narration by saying:

Ibn-ul-Mubarak was asked about the explanation of this narration so

---

165. Majmu'a Al-Fatawa.

166. Ibn Majah: 224.

he said, 'It is not as you think, seeking knowledge is only obligatory if a man enters into a situation among the affairs of his religion, so he asks about it until he knows it.' Al-Busairi said, 'The intent of knowledge here is what is imperative for the servant to learn e.g. awareness of the Creator and knowledge of His Oneness, the prophetic mission of His Messenger, and the manner of the prayer's performance; Indeed the learning of this is an individual obligation.'[167]

The ruling referred to as "obligatory" has two distinguished types and they are as follows:

- Individual Obligation: it is an obligation made binding on every single Muslim who is of sound mind and has reached the age of maturity from both male and female. No one is exempt from the obligation fundamentally.

- Communal Obligation: It is an obligation made binding on the community in general. The intent of this is that if someone or a group among the community embarks upon the fulfillment of this obligation it removes the burden from the remainder of the community. However, if no one takes on the responsibility then the entire community is sinful until the responsibility is executed.

As relates to seeking knowledge of the religion, then both types (of obligation) are applicable, as there is an aspect of the religion that is an individual obligation to learn and another aspect that is a communal obligation to obtain. This leads us to an important question; what aspect of the religion is an individual obligation, insomuch that if it's abandoned the Muslim becomes sinful? And what aspects are considered a communal obligation to the extent that if no one is burdened with the responsibility the entire community becomes sinful?

Sheikh Salih al-Fawzan states:

What is obligatory for every individual to learn, consequently being no excuse for the one who is ignorant concerning it; it is that which the religion cannot be established except by way of it, i.e. the five pillars

---

167. Misbah Az-Zujajah.

of Islam and they are the two testimonies, performing the prayers, paying the annual charity, fasting during Ramadan, and pilgrimage to Allah's House. It is not permissible for any Muslim to be ignorant of these affairs, on the contrary it is incumbent that he learns them. For instance, learning the two testimonies is—in reality—learning Islam's creed. The Muslim learns the Islamic creed in order to enact it. Moreover he learns what conflicts with it in order to shun it as this is implied by the two testimonies.

Likewise he learns the prayer, its prerequisites, its obligations, and its recommended acts. These affairs are incumbent to be learned with detail, it is not for a person to strictly pray while he doesn't know the rulings of the prayer. How can a person perform an action while he is unaware of the action that he enacts?! How can he establish the prayer while being unaware of its rulings? It is incumbent to learn the rulings of the prayer and its invalidators. In addition, learning the rulings of the annual charity, the rulings of the fast, and the rulings of the pilgrimage. If a person wants to make the pilgrimage it is binding upon him to learn its rulings and the rulings of umrah (i.e. the lesser pilgrimage) in order to perform this act of worship according to its legislation. This is the category of which no one is excused on account of ignorance and it is dubbed the individual obligation upon every Muslim.

The second category related to knowledge is that which is additional to that from the Legislative Rulings in which the Islamic Nation stands in need of amassing, but is seldomly needed by every individual. For instance the rulings on selling merchandise, the rulings on transactions, the rulings on endowments, the rulings on inheritance, the rulings on bequeathals, the rulings on marriage, and the rulings on penal punishments. This is incumbent upon the Islamic Nation (i.e. its acquisition); however, it is not obligatory upon every individual from this nation to learn. On the contrary, when it is learned by whoever acquires it—the intended among the scholars—then this suffices due to them establishing what the Muslims are in need of as relates to judgments, verdicts, education, etc. This is referred to as the communal obligation; if one embarks upon fulfilling the responsibility it suffices in removing the sin from the remainder (of the community). But when it is abandoned by the entire community, the entire community is sinful.[168]

---

168. Sharh Thalathat-ul-Usul.

SPEAKING ABOUT AFFAIRS OF THE RELIGION WITHOUT KNOWLEDGE IS SINFUL

Among the gravest of sins is to speak about Allah or the guidance He revealed from above the seven heavens while being ignorant of what you say. In other words, the Muslim who believes in Allah and the Last Day doesn't say what he thinks, or how he feels about Allah and His guidance, on the contrary he speaks what he knows from what he obtained of knowledge from Allah's Book or from the prophetic traditions of His Messenger ﷺ anything aside from that is conjecture which doesn't aid the truth in anyway. Thus speaking about affairs of the religion is prohibited and there is no differing in that regard.

Allah says that which is rendered into the English language as:

$$ قُلْ إِنَّمَا حَرَّمَ رَبِّيَ ٱلْفَوَٰحِشَ مَا ظَهَرَ مِنْهَا وَمَا بَطَنَ وَٱلْإِثْمَ وَٱلْبَغْىَ بِغَيْرِ ٱلْحَقِّ وَأَن تُشْرِكُوا۟ بِٱللَّهِ مَا لَمْ يُنَزِّلْ بِهِۦ سُلْطَٰنًا وَأَن تَقُولُوا۟ عَلَى ٱللَّهِ مَا لَا تَعْلَمُونَ $$

Say: My Lord has only prohibited immorality, what is apparent and concealed of it, sinfulness, transgression without due right, that you associate a partner in worship with Allah of that which no authority was given, and that you say about Allah that which you have no knowledge. [Al-A'raf: 33]

This verse's meaning is manifest and overtly clear. It is unequivocal in stating the prohibition for speaking about Islam without knowledge as the ramifications for doing such can be disastrous.

Sheikh-ul-Islam ibn Taymiyyah said:

These aforementioned things are prohibited in every legislation (of prophets prior to Muhammad ﷺ). Allah sent all of the messengers with this prohibition and nothing of it was ever made permissible. For this reason it was revealed within this Meccan chapter and the prohibition of whatever is besides that was negated. So He only prohibited other things after it e.g. blood (poured forth from a slaughtered animal), a carcass, and the flesh of swine, He prohibited this in a circumstance aside from another circumstance;

however, their prohibition is not in the absolute sense (like that which is mentioned in the verse).

For example, intoxicants; it is made permissible in order to ward off choking by agreement (i.e. of the scholars). It's also permissible to repel thirst (in an abnormal circumstance in which there is no water and the person is dying from thirst) as is contained within one of two opinions among the scholars. As for those who do not make it permissible (i.e. in this abnormal circumstance) they say that it doesn't quench thirst and this is the way of Imam Ahmad. Thus the affair is unresolved as relates to it quenching thirst, thus if it is known that it will repel thirst then it is permissible without doubt, just as the flesh of swine repels starvation and the dire need concerning thirst that which is perceived to cause destruction (to the thirsty person) is more of an necessity than hunger. On account of this, it is permissible to consume impurities when (dying of) thirst (during a drought) without dispute. Hence it either repels thirst and if not there is no allowance for anything of it in that regard.[169]

To recap; Sheikh-ul-Islam ibn Taymiyyah is expounding on the grave magnitude of the sins mentioned within the verse. They're of such a magnitude that these things were prohibited in every single legislation delivered by every messenger due to what they produced of great harm regardless of which period of time they are present or among which group of people on the face of the earth they are affixed to. In contrast to other sins; although the fundamental ruling to them is prohibition, there are circumstances that may arise where that prohibition is dropped momentarily as Sheikh-ul-Islam explained in order to repel an eminent harm.

Ibn Qayyim al-Jawziyyah said:

As for speaking about Allah without knowledge it is the most severe of prohibited acts and gravest of sins. On account of that it is mentioned as the fourth category among the categories of prohibited acts that every legislation had agreement with. So they are not made permissible on account of an abnormal circumstances (which makes necessary they're implementation in order to repel an impending harm), on the contrary they cannot be anything except prohibited and that is not the case with dead meat, blood, or the flesh of swine that can be made permissible on account of a circumstance aside from the norm.

---

169. Majmu'a Al-Fatawa: 14/470-471.

Thus the prohibited matters are of two types; a prohibition (of a matter) inherently thus it is not allowed under any circumstance, and a prohibition whose impermissible nature is contingent upon a certain time (and circumstance) aside from another time (in which the circumstance differs). Thus the Exalted said about the inherently prohibited, **'Say: My Lord has only prohibited immorality, what is apparent and concealed of it, sinfulness, transgression without due right.'** Then He transitions to the graver among them, So He says, **'that you associate a partner in worship with Allah of that which no authority was given.'** Then He moves to the next of what is grave, so He says, **'and that you say about Allah that which you have no knowledge.'** This is the gravest of sins with Allah and the most severe as it is inclusive of inventing lies against Allah, attribution to Him what is not befitting of Him, altering His religion and changing it, negation of what He affirmed and affirmation of what He negates, materialization of what He declared false and declaring to be true what is actually false, hostility for whoever supports Him and support for whoever holds hostility towards Him, love for whatever He hates and hate for whatever He loves, describing Him with what is not befitting as pertains to His essence (i.e. self), attributes, speech, and actions.

Therefore there isn't within the classifications of the prohibited that which is greater with Allah than it and more severe in sin than it. It is the foundation of polytheism and disbelief, upon it innovation and misguidance are based. Thus every misguided innovation in the religion its foundation is speech about Allah without knowledge.[170]

This point becomes clear when examining the claims of the previous nations. For instance, the claim that Allah has the name "The Father" which suggests that He is a progenitor, this without a doubt is speech about Allah without knowledge. The claim that Allah, Jesus, and the holy spirit are three personalities making up one God is clearly speech about Allah without knowledge. The claim that Allah is love which asserts that Allah loves every person on the face of the earth and has no hate is speech about Allah without knowledge. The claim that Allah created the heavens and the earth in seven days and then rested is speech about Allah without knowledge. The claim that Allah is a man of war, and in the Hebrew Israelite teachings a black man is undoubtedly speech about Allah without knowledge. The claim that the Descendants of Israel are Allah's chosen

---

170. Madarij-us-Salikin.

people and the only people beloved to Allah at the exclusion of the rest of humanity is speech about Allah without knowledge. And whatever else that is uttered about Allah that is absurd and ignorant which lowers Allah's grandeur and magnificence with the creation and diverts them away from Him and His rights made binding upon them, and Allah knows best.

EVIDENCE ON THE BLAMEWORTHINESS OF ACTING UPON IGNORANCE

يَـٰٓأَيُّهَا ٱلنَّاسُ كُلُوا۟ مِمَّا فِى ٱلْأَرْضِ حَلَـٰلًا طَيِّبًا وَلَا تَتَّبِعُوا۟ خُطُوَٰتِ ٱلشَّيْطَـٰنِ إِنَّهُۥ لَكُمْ عَدُوٌّ مُّبِينٌ ﴿١٦٨﴾ إِنَّمَا يَأْمُرُكُم بِٱلسُّوٓءِ وَٱلْفَحْشَآءِ وَأَن تَقُولُوا۟ عَلَى ٱللَّهِ مَا لَا تَعْلَمُونَ ﴿١٦٩﴾

O Mankind! Eat from what is within the earth that is lawful and pure and do not follow the footsteps of the devil, undoubtedly he is to you all a clear enemy. He only instructs you with evil, immorality, and to say about Allah that which you have no knowledge. [Al-Baqarah: 168-169]

وَإِذَا جَآءَهُمْ أَمْرٌ مِّنَ ٱلْأَمْنِ أَوِ ٱلْخَوْفِ أَذَاعُوا۟ بِهِۦ وَلَوْ رَدُّوهُ إِلَى ٱلرَّسُولِ وَإِلَىٰٓ أُو۟لِى ٱلْأَمْرِ مِنْهُمْ لَعَلِمَهُ ٱلَّذِينَ يَسْتَنۢبِطُونَهُۥ مِنْهُمْ وَلَوْلَا فَضْلُ ٱللَّهِ عَلَيْكُمْ وَرَحْمَتُهُۥ لَٱتَّبَعْتُمُ ٱلشَّيْطَـٰنَ إِلَّا قَلِيلًا

And when there comes to them an affair related to safety or fear they circulate it. If they had returned the matter back to the messenger and those in authority among them, those who derive proper rulings among them would have known it. And if not for Allah's favor and mercy upon you surely you would've followed the devil except a minority (among you). [An-Nisa: 83]

وَلَا تَقُولُوا۟ لِمَا تَصِفُ أَلْسِنَتُكُمُ ٱلْكَذِبَ هَـٰذَا حَلَـٰلٌ وَهَـٰذَا حَرَامٌ لِّتَفْتَرُوا۟ عَلَى ٱللَّهِ ٱلْكَذِبَ إِنَّ ٱلَّذِينَ يَفْتَرُونَ عَلَى ٱللَّهِ ٱلْكَذِبَ لَا يُفْلِحُونَ

And say not that which your tongues put forward

lyingly, 'this is lawful and this is prohibited' in order to invent a lie against Allah. Indeed those who invent lies against Allah will not be successful. [An-Nahl: 116]

$$ وَلَا تَقْفُ مَا لَيْسَ لَكَ بِهِۦ عِلْمٌ إِنَّ ٱلسَّمْعَ وَٱلْبَصَرَ وَٱلْفُؤَادَ كُلُّ أُو۟لَٰٓئِكَ كَانَ عَنْهُ مَسْـُٔولًا $$

And do not pursue that which you have no knowledge of, indeed the hearing, sight, and hearts all of which will be questioned. [Al-Isra: 36]

$$ بَلِ ٱتَّبَعَ ٱلَّذِينَ ظَلَمُوٓا۟ أَهْوَآءَهُم بِغَيْرِ عِلْمٍ فَمَن يَهْدِى مَنْ أَضَلَّ ٱللَّهُ وَمَا لَهُم مِّن نَّٰصِرِينَ $$

Nay, those that act oppressively follow their desires without knowledge, thus who will guide whomever Allah allows to go astray? For them there is no helper. [Ar-Rum: 29]

$$ وَمَا يَتَّبِعُ أَكْثَرُهُمْ إِلَّا ظَنًّا إِنَّ ٱلظَّنَّ لَا يُغْنِى مِنَ ٱلْحَقِّ شَيْـًٔا إِنَّ ٱللَّهَ عَلِيمٌۢ بِمَا يَفْعَلُونَ $$

And most of them follow nothing but conjecture. Surely conjecture doesn't benefit the truth in the least. Undoubtedly Allah is All-Knower of what you do. [Yunus: 36]

$$ وَمَا لَهُم بِهِۦ مِنْ عِلْمٍ إِن يَتَّبِعُونَ إِلَّا ٱلظَّنَّ وَإِنَّ ٱلظَّنَّ لَا يُغْنِى مِنَ ٱلْحَقِّ شَيْـًٔا $$

And there is no knowledge with them, indeed they follow conjecture. Surely conjecture doesn't benefit the truth in the least. [An-Najm: 28]

$$ فَسْـَٔلُوٓا۟ أَهْلَ ٱلذِّكْرِ إِن كُنتُمْ لَا تَعْلَمُونَ $$

So ask the people of knowledge if you don't know. [An-Nahl: 43, and Al-Anbiya: 7]

Jabir ibn Abdullah said: "We departed on a journey and (while traveling) a man was stricken with a rock resulting in a wound on his head.

Sometime thereafter he had a wet dream, so he asked his comrades by saying, 'Do you all find it possible for me to apply the concession of tayammum?' They said, 'We cannot find for you a concession while you are able to use water.' Consequently he took a bath and died as a result, so the Prophet ﷺ was informed about him and he consequently said, 'They killed him, may Allah kill them, why didn't they ask if they did not know? The only cure for ignorance is a question. Tayammun would have sufficed him.'"[171]

Abdullah ibn Amr ibn al-Aas narrates the Prophet's ﷺ statement: "Allah will not seize knowledge by snatching it away from His servants; however, He will take knowledge by taking the scholars until there doesn't remain any scholar. Consequently the people will take from the leaders of the ignorant. Thus they will be asked, resulting in them issuing verdicts without knowledge. So they are astray and they'll lead others astray."[172]

Abu Saeed al-Khudri narrates Allah's Prophet's ﷺ speech: "There was among those before you a man who killed ninety nine men. So he asked about the most knowledgeable of the people of the earth, resulting in him being directed towards a devout worshiper. So he went to him and said that he had killed ninety nine men and if there was any repentance for him. So the worshiper said, 'No.' Consequently the man killed him and completed 100 killings. Thereafter, he (again) asked about the most knowledgeable of the people within the land and was directed to a scholar. So, he (went to him and) said that he killed 100 men and if there was for him repentance. The scholar replied, 'Yes, and who would stand as an obstruction between him and repentance? Depart heading towards the land of such and such, certainly within it is a people that worship Allah, so worship Him along with them. Additionally, do not return to your land for indeed it is an evil land.' So he departed until he reached the halfway mark of the route when death came to him. Hence the angels of mercy and of punishment disputed over him. The angels of mercy said, 'He came as a repenter with his heart turning towards Allah.' The angels of punishment said, 'He never committed any good.' Then an angel came in the form of a man so they placed him between

---

171. Abu Dawud: 336.

172. Bukhari: 100 and Muslim: 2673.

148

them (as a judge). He said, 'measure what is between the two portions of earth (from the point of death to whence he came and to where he was headed), as he belongs to whichever is the closest of the two.' So they measured it and found that he was closer to the land he intended (from his journey), so the angels of mercy took him."[173]

RECOGNIZING THE JURIST AND SCHOLAR

The author of *The Six Principles* said, "Consequently, knowledge that Allah made binding upon His creation and praised, no one uttered it except a heretic or one mentally challenged. Moreover whoever disapproved of, and held hostility towards it along with warning against and prohibiting it then he is the jurist and or scholar" which illustrates the condition of the Muslims in his time which has only become worse in modern times. Today many people are held as scholars in Islam for varying reasons, e.g. eloquent and charismatic speech, possesses a degree from an Islamic university, outer appearance that is perceive by many Muslims to be the appearance of a scholar, popularity on social media platforms, etc; that don't necessitate being a scholar. As a result many are led astray by people who are inadequate in terms of knowledge and conveyance. In contrast to those who are scholars or proficient teachers who may not be as charismatic when speaking, or may not hold a degree, etc. All of this stems from a lack of understanding as relates to what a person should be proficient in as relates to knowledge, in order to be deemed a scholar in Islam.

Without a doubt the person must know in detail the aspects of knowledge made binding upon every Muslim to know (as previously mentioned); however, his knowledge must exceed that in order to be qualified as someone who can pass rulings on actions, issue religious verdicts, and exercise independent judgment by usage of Islamic Fiqh related jurist principles and guidelines. Thus the person must have other aspects of knowledge with him in order to be deemed a scholar in Islam. Sheikh Muhammad ibn Salih al-Uthaymin in his book *Al-Usool Min Ilm Al-Usool* mentions that which the person must be proficient in, to be

---

173. Bukhari: 3470 and Muslim: 2766.

considered a scholar in Islam, and they are as follows:

- As relates to the Islamic Legislative Evidence, the person must know what is needed to exercise independent judgment, specifically the verses of the Quran dealing with *ahkam* (rulings), and the authentic narrations in that regard.

- He should know what is connected to the authentication of a narration (hadith) or its weakness e.g., knowledge of the chain of transmission, the men within the chain, etc.

- He should know the abrogations of text (i.e. what text abrogates another), and the affairs of consensus (*ijmaa*) so that he doesn't make a judgment by usage of what is abrogated nor in contradiction to the consensus.

- He should know the evidence, i.e. what causes the differing of a judgment by way of it. For example, knowing the difference between a specified statement and a restricted statement, etc; so that no judgment is made in contrast to that.

- Knowledge of the Arabic language and Usool Fiqh that which is connected to what verbal expressions signify as pertains to general and specific (speech), restricted and unrestricted (speech), definite and inexact speech, etc; in order to make judgments in accordance with the significations.

- That he has the ability which enables him to derive rulings from the evidence.

These are qualities that the common muslim unacquainted with knowledge is unable to determine. Thus there is no way he can determine who a scholar is or is not. Unfortunately in this time you have people doing just that, i.e. claiming someone is a scholar who is not, and declaring authentic scholars to be ignorant. We seek Allah's aid from being led astray.

The Fifth Principle

Author

The clarification of Allah—The Glorified—concerning His awliyya, along with differentiation between them and those who resemble them from Allah's enemies, the hypocrites, and the immoral. Sufficient with regards to illustration of this is a verse in Ali-Imran (31) and it is His statement: "Say! If you love Allah then follow me, consequently Allah will love you..." Moreover the verse in Al-Maa'idah (54): "O you who believe! Whoever among you that turns away from his religion, will result in Allah coming with a people that He will love and they will love him..." Likewise the verse in Yunus (63-62): "Undoubtedly the awliyya of Allah shall not be overcome with fear nor shall they grieve. Those who believed and exemplified taqwa."

Thereafter this affair—with an abundance of those that feign knowledge among the guiders/mentors of the creation and the preservers of the Islamic Legislation—started to perceive—as relates to the awliyya—that it was necessary for them to abandon conformity to the messengers, therefore whoever followed the messengers was not among the awliyya. Furthermore (they perceived) that it was necessary—i.e. for the awliyya—to abandon jihad, hence whoever participated therein was not among them. Lastly (they also perceived) it to be necessary to abandon Al-Iman and Taqwa, so whoever committed himself to Al-Iman and Taqwa was not among them O our Lord! We ask You for pardon and protection, indeed You are the All Hearing of invocations.

This principle is specific to Allah's *awliyya*, i.e. who they are and what their characteristics are. This clarification is of great importance today like it was during the time of the author on account of the affair becoming even more confused today than from what occurred during the author's time. Not only do people allege that some personalities that fanaticism is held for are *awliyya*, but there are people today that allege that they themselves are awliyya, shamelessly. This self praise and aggrandizement is specific to people of our time; unfortunately, on account of people's ignorance they affirm the claims of these people, support them, and propagate their self serving agendas to the detriment of the Islamic Nation.

WHAT IS INTENDED BY AWLIYYA?

First, *awliyya* is an Arabic word which is a plural to the word *wali* (ally). Wali has several different meanings linguistically which are easily distinguishable based on the context of its usage. The context in which it's being used in this principle is also clear and has been defined by the people of knowledge.

Sheikh-ul-Islam ibn Taymiyyah said: "So the *awliyya* they are the possessors of taqwa, the believers."[174] He also said: "Thus everyone who believes in Allah and His Messenger and fears Allah, then he is among the *awliyya* of Allah."[175]

Al Hafidh ibn Hajr al-Asqalani said: "The intent of a *wali* of Allah is the knowledgeable person concerning Allah, the persistent person upon His obedience, and the sincere person as relates to worship of Him."[176]

Sheikh Muhammad Amaan al-Jami said: "Whoever Allah guides to faith and righteous actions, he is a *wali*."[177]

Sheikh Muhammad ibn Salih al-Uthaymin said: "They are those that

---

174. Al-Furqan.

175. Majmu'a Al-Fatawa: 3/417.

176. Fath-ul-Bari.

177. Sharh Usul-us-Sittah.

believe in Him, fear Him, and are upright upon His religion."[178]

Sheikh Salih Alish-Sheikh said:

> The *wali* with Ahlus Sunnah wal Jamaa'ah is defined as every believer and possessor of taqwa with exclusion to prophets. This is the *wali* as pertains to religious technical terms with Ahlus Sunnah i.e., the *wali* is everyone that has faith and taqwa.[179]

This definition stated by the people of knowledge is directly derived from an unambiguous statement of Allah in Sura Yunus often quoted by them. Within this statement Allah, the All-Knower of the seen and unseen, defines who they are resulting in the scholars simply conveying what He elucidated. Allah says about the *awliyya* that which is rendered into English to mean:

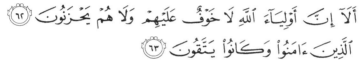

Undoubtedly the *awliyya* of Allah shall not be overcome with fear nor shall they grieve. Those who believed and exemplified taqwa. [62-63]

Ibn Kathir said: "The Exalted informs us about His *awliyya* (allies). They are those who believe and exemplify *taqwa* just as their Lord explained. Hence, whoever is a possessor of taqwa is to Allah a *wali*."

In light of the aforementioned, in order to fully comprehend the definition of wali we must understand the definition of *taqwa*. As a person cannot be a *wali* of Allah without being a possessor of *taqwa* as defined by Allah.

WHAT IS TAQWA?

Asim al-Ahwal reports Bakr al-Muzani's speech:

---

178. Sharh Usul-us-Sittah.

179. Sharh Arba'in an-Nawawiyyah.

During the tribulation of ibn Ash'ath, Talq ibn Habib (a *Tabi'ee*) said, 'Be on guard from it (i.e. the tribulation) by way of *taqwa*.' Consequently it was said to him, 'Describe to us *taqwa*?' So he replied, 'Actions according to Allah's obedience, upon light from Allah, hoping for the rewards of Allah. Likewise to abandon sinfulness to Allah, upon light from Allah, fearing the punishment of Allah.'[180]

Imam Adh-Dhabi stated, while commenting on Talq ibn Habib's statement:

More concisely put, there is no *taqwa* without action, and there is no action without careful consideration from knowledge and conformity. None of this is beneficial without *ikhlas* (sincerity) to Allah. This is not for the purpose of being said that so-and-so abandoned sins due to the light of comprehension, because avoidance of sins requires knowledge of them; on the contrary, abandonment is on account of fear from Allah not for the purpose of (mere) abandonment of it. Consequently, whoever perseveres upon this undoubtedly achieves success.[181]

Thus the one who possesses taqwa has several characteristics which must be assembled in order for it to be a source of benefit:

- Actions in accordance with Allah's command.
- Abandonment of whatsoever Allah prohibits.
- A foundation rooted in firm knowledge as relates to enactment and abandonment.
- All are done purely, strictly, and sincerely for Allah.

The one who combines these things is one who possesses taqwa, and Allah knows best.

THE AWLIYYA VARY IN TERMS OF STATUS AND RANK

Sheikh Salih Alish-Sheikh said:

Faith and Taqwa differentiate in precedence. Faith increases and decreases and its people rival in superiority (in terms of who is higher in faith). Likewise *taqwa*, its people rival in superiority as relates to it (i.e. in terms of practical implementation and who is more plentiful in

---

180. Siyar Alam An-Nubala.

181. Siyar Alam An-Nubala.

that regard). As a result, the description of *walayah*, its people rival for precedence in that regard as well. So the *awliyya* are not upon the same level; however, quite often the Islamic technical definition for wali is a believer who enhances *taqwa* according to his ability, yet someone who has something of faith and something of taqwa is not considered a *wali* even though every believer and possessor of *taqwa* has *walayah* accordingly.

Thus the difference between the word *wali* and *walayah*; walayah is Allah's love and assistance for His servant in accordance with what is with him of faith and *taqwa*. As for the *wali*, the verse indicates that whoever has within him faith and taqwa is among the *awliyya*; however, in terms of the technical definition it is said that the *awliyya* are the righteous servants that complete their *taqwa* according to their ability, thus whoever mixes righteous actions with evil deeds does not enter into it.[182]

Sheikh Muhammad Amaan al-Jami said: "The *awliyya* (allies) vary with each other in terms of their level and nearness to Allah. Likewise in their love for Allah's sake and their exaltation of His legislation similar to the enemies of Allah varying with each other in terms of their enmity."[183]

This reality is understood in light of the definition of *wali*. The *wali* is a person with faith and *taqwa* and the faith of a believer fluctuates. It increases at times and decreases. Likewise one's steadfastness in implementation of righteous deeds; one may be diligent in observing—for instance—the obligatory fast of Ramadan; however, when it comes to the voluntary fast one person may be successful in fasting the three white days of each month, whereas another person increases upon that and fasts every 2nd and 5th day of the week along with the white days. Another person may not fast except on occasions like the Day of Arafat and the 9th and 10th of Muharram. Thus each person varies as relates to his implementation and faith necessitating one person being closer to Allah than the other. Moreover, a person may be diligent in observing not only obligatory but also voluntary acts at times, but may fall short at other times with persistence in implementation of voluntary acts due to

---

182. Sharh Al-Furqan.

183. Sharh Usul-us-Sittah.

a decrease in faith. In contrast to another person who may implement what is strictly obligatory, but at some point increases in good deeds which consequently causes an increase in faith. The point; the awliyya are not all on the same level as the scholars allude to, their levels vary based on the varying levels of faith and taqwa, and Allah knows best. A simple example is the varying levels of the prophets. A messenger is on another level than one who is strictly a prophet.

Sheikh Muhammad Amaan al-Jami said:

> The prophets are the foremost in rank of the *awliyya*, and it is not as the ignorant Sufis' claim that the awliyya are something separate from the prophets and messengers. In other words, as pertains to the claims of the Sufis the term awliyya isn't applied to the prophets and messengers. So this is a mistake in perception, rather the prophets are foremost in ranking of the *awliyaa*. Furthermore, among (the foremost of) the prophets are the messengers, among the foremost of the messengers are the possessors of firm resolve (i.e. Nuh, Ibrahim, Musa, Esa, and Muhammad), thereafter their leader without restriction i.e. the leader of the descendants of Adam; Muhammad ﷺ as he is the leader of the *awliyya*, the first of them, and the most virtuous of them without restriction.[184]

Note: The point of Sheikh Muhammad Amaan al-Jami concerning the levels of the *awliyya* being varied is explicitly clear; however, within his explanation the reader may notice how he clashes with what Sheikh Salih Alish-Sheikh said concerning the definition of *wali*. Sheikh Salih excluded the prophets from being amongst the *awliyya*, in contrast to Sheikh Muhammad Amaan. In addition, Sheikh Muhammad Amaan states that this understanding is from the claims of the Sufis consequently prompting the question to be asked, did Sheikh Salih make a mistake? Was he in accordance with the deviances of the Sufis? These questions answered with a simple statement are no; however, detail is needed in order for the reader to benefit.

Sometimes there arises points of differing among the scholars of Ahlus Sunnah as pertains to *ijtihad* related issues. In some issues you may find that the people of innovation and desire may hold the same opinion

---

184. Sharh Usul-us-Sittah.

as a group among the scholars of Ahlus Sunnah in an issue in which they differ. Nonetheless, it doesn't necessitate that the statement of this group of scholars is now a deviant opinion on account of a sect among the people of innovation being in agreement with that opinion. The point is that this issue is one of those types of issues and Sheikh Salih alludes to this in his explanation to *Al-Furqan* where he states, "On account of this a group among the people of knowledge define *wali* as every believer and possessor of taqwa that is not a prophet." Examples in this regard are many.

THE AWLIYYA ARE BELOVED TO ALLAH

Abu Huraira narrates the Messenger's ﷺ statement:

> *Allah, the Exalted said, 'Whoever shows enmity to a wali of mines I declare war against him. My servant will never cease to become near to me with anything more beloved to Me than what I made binding upon him. Likewise my servant doesn't cease becoming near to Me by way of voluntary acts until I love him. Thus I become his hearing by which he ears, his sight by which he sees, his hand by which he grasps, his foot by which he walks. If he asks me, I give to him; and when he seeks refuge, I shelter him. I do not hesitate in anything that I do like my hesitation with the life of the believer, as he hates death and I hate to disappoint him.'*[185]

This authentic narration, its meaning is tremendous. Statements within it are unambiguous as relates to the status of the *wali*. Undoubtedly, we learn that the *wali* is beloved to Allah. This derivation is extracted from some statements within the narration, among them is the following:

Whoever shows enmity to a wali of mines I declare war against him.

This statement is explicit in its meaning. It illustrates the status of the *wali* of Allah with Allah, insomuch that he is beloved to Allah, to the extent

---

185. Bukhari: 6502.

that Allah punishes the person who shows hostility towards His *wali*.

Al Hafidh ibn Hajr al-Asqalani said:

> Al-Fakihani said, 'Within this is a severe threat because he who Allah wages war against He destroys. It's a powerful figurative expression on account that whoever hates whomever Allah loves disobeys Allah, and whoever disobeys Allah opposes Him, and whoever opposes Him destroys himself. So if this is firmly established from the perspective of enmity then it is established from the perspective of support. In other words, whoever supports a *wali* from Allah's *awliyya*, Allah honors him.'[186]

Sheikh Muhammad al-Uthaymin said the following when enumerating the benefits derived from the narration: "Enmity towards Allah's *awliyya* is among the major sins due to His statement 'I declare war against him' this is a particular punishment for a particular action, thus this action is among the major sins."[187]

Likewise my servant doesn't cease becoming near to Me by way of voluntary acts until I love him.

This is explicit in meaning, Allah states, "until I love him" showing us the means to obtaining His love. There is no greater means than implementation of that which He made binding upon man to enact. Subsequent to that is implementation of recommended acts, i.e. that which is not binding, thus a person is not sinful if they are abandoned; however, if implemented the doer is rewarded insomuch that it is the means to Allah's love for him.

Ibn Rajab al-Hanbali said:

> When He mentioned that hostility towards His *awliyya* is actually waging war against Himself, He also mentioned thereafter the characteristics of His *awliyya* to which He forbade hostility towards and made binding support/loyalty towards. So He mentioned what is utilized to be brought close to Him, as the foundation of loyalty/support is nearness and the foundation of hostility is distance/farness. Hence, the *awliyya* of Allah are those who seek nearness to Him by utilization

---

186. Fath-ul-Bari.

187. Sharh Al-Araba'in.

of what brings them closer to Him. In contrast, His enemies are those that distance themselves from Him with actions that necessitate their expulsion and distance from Him.

Consequently, He has divided His *awliyya* into two categories. The first of the two is whoever seeks nearness to him by executing the prescribed actions. This includes enactment of obligatory acts and abandonment of the prohibited on account that all of this is what Allah prescribed for His servants to carry out. The second of the two is whoever seeks nearness with what is subsequent to the prescribed i.e., with voluntary acts.[188]

Al Hafidh ibn Hajr al-Asqalani said:

On the apparent Allah's love for the servant occurs by the servant's inseparableness to the seeking nearness by way of recommended acts, it becomes problematic on account of what proceeded first that being the prescribed actions being the most beloved acts of worship which by it nearness to Allah is sought, so how doesn't it result in love? The answer is that the intent of recommended acts is that which is (like) a container for the prescribed acts, encompassing and completing them.

Furthermore, this is supported within the chain of transmission of Abu Umamah (which says), 'Son of Adam! You will never reach what is with Me except by performing what I have prescribed upon you.' Al-Fakihani said, 'The meaning of the narration is that when he performs the prescribed acts and is persistent in coming with voluntary acts from the prayer, fasting, and others aside from that; they eventually lead towards Allah's love.'[189]

Sheikh Salih al-Fawzan said:

So this indicates the seeking nearness to Allah can only be by way of what He legislated regardless if it's obligatory or recommended. Obligatory things like the five daily prayers, the zakat, the fast of Ramadan, pilgrimage to the sacred house of Allah, and maintaining family ties. These are the obligatory acts, as for the recommended as relates to voluntary acts of obedience (they are) for instance, the night prayer, the forenoon prayer, and the voluntary prayers connected to the five obligatory prayers. These are voluntary and are not made binding, they are strictly recommended and complete the prescribed acts as they are an increase in good.

---

188. Jami-ul-Uloom wal Hikm.

189. Fath-ul-Bari.

Therefore it is not benefitting for a Muslim to be restricted to implementation of the obligatory, on the contrary he should increase with voluntary acts as well, as this is the *wali* of Allah, he who seeks nearness to Allah with obligatory and voluntary acts. Allah said, 'My servant will never cease to become near to me with anything more beloved to Me' indicates that Allah loves righteous deeds just as He hates evil deeds. Moreover, Allah loves, hates, despises, and gets angry in accordance with the manner befitting His majesty."

The Sheikh also said: "'Until I love him' this is a firm establishment/ affirmation of (the quality) love being attributed to Allah. Thus He loves righteous servants, and righteous actions. Likewise it indicates that righteous actions are a means to Allah's love for the servant, so if you want Allah to love you then be plentiful in enactment of acts of obedience. Additionally, if you want Allah to love you, then follow the Messenger.[190]

As for the remainder of the narration and what it entails, Sheikh Abdul Muhsin al-Abbad lists some of the benefits derived from it in his explanation to the 40 Hadith of Imam An-Nawawi. They are as follows:

- An elucidation of the virtues of Allah's *awliyya* and the danger of hostility towards them.
- The loyalty, love, and support (*walaya*) of Allah is achieved by implementation of the obligatory acts and the voluntary.
- The most beloved of what nearness to Allah is sought by is the performance of obligatory acts.
- Affirmation of Allah's quality/attribute love.
- The variance of (virtue for) actions pertains to Allah's love of them (i.e. obligatory acts are more beloved thus are more virtuous).
- Enacting voluntary acts after the obligatory brings about the love of Allah.
- Whoever achieves the love of Allah, He guides him as pertains to his hearing, sight, grasping/holding, and walking.
- Allah's love obtains for the servant a response to his invocation and protection from his fears.

---

190. Al-Minha Ar-Rabbaniyyah.

- Allah's reward due to the servant is by responding to his requests and protection from his fears.

The erudite scholar, Muhammad ibn Salih al-Uthaymin also mentioned benefits derived from this narration in his explanation to Imam An-Nawawi's 40 Hadith. Some benefits are repetitively mentioned, thus there's no need to repeat them lest I fall into redundancy. However, I will mention those that weren't listed by Sheikh Abdul Muhsin, they are as follows:

- Hostility towards the awliyya of Allah is a major sin on account of the threat of war waged against whoever does so.
- Affirmation of Allah's action of waging war against someone.
- An urge to implement voluntary acts.
- The honor Allah holds for His awliyya.
- The commands of Allah are categorized into two categories: prescribed and voluntary. The prescribed acts consist of those which take the ruling of obligatory or prohibited, the voluntary acts take the ruling of recommended.

CHARACTERISTICS OF THOSE LOVED BY ALLAH
THE MUHSIN

وَأَنفِقُوا۟ فِى سَبِيلِ ٱللَّهِ وَلَا تُلْقُوا۟ بِأَيْدِيكُمْ إِلَى ٱلتَّهْلُكَةِ وَأَحْسِنُوٓا۟ إِنَّ ٱللَّهَ يُحِبُّ ٱلْمُحْسِنِينَ

And spend in the path of Allah and do not throw yourselves into destruction with your own hands. Also enact good, undoubtedly Allah loves the _Muhsinoon_. [Al-Baqarah: 195]

ٱلَّذِينَ يُنفِقُونَ فِى ٱلسَّرَّآءِ وَٱلضَّرَّآءِ وَٱلْكَٰظِمِينَ ٱلْغَيْظَ وَٱلْعَافِينَ عَنِ ٱلنَّاسِ وَٱللَّهُ يُحِبُّ ٱلْمُحْسِنِينَ

Those who spend during prosperity and adversity, withhold their anger, and who pardon, surely Allah

loves the *Muhsinoon*. [Ali-Imran: 134]

$$ثُمَّ ٱتَّقَوا۟ وَّأَحْسَنُوا۟ وَٱللَّهُ يُحِبُّ ٱلْمُحْسِنِينَ$$

...and fear Allah and enact good, certainly Allah loves the *Muhsinoon*. [Al-Ma'idah: 93]

THE TAWWAB

$$إِنَّ ٱللَّهَ يُحِبُّ ٱلتَّوَّٰبِينَ$$

...certainly Allah loves the *tawwabun*... [Al Baqarah: 222]

The *tawwab* is he who makes *taubah*, and *taubah* is to return to Allah's obedience after leaving it. It's done solely for Allah's pleasure along with remorse for the sin committed. Hence the tawwab is he who is plentiful in making repentance.

THE MUTTAQI

$$بَلَىٰ مَنْ أَوْفَىٰ بِعَهْدِهِۦ وَٱتَّقَىٰ فَإِنَّ ٱللَّهَ يُحِبُّ ٱلْمُتَّقِينَ$$

Of course, whoever fulfills his pledge and has taqwa, then surely Allah loves the *muttaqoon*. [Ali-Imran: 76]

$$فَأَتِمُّوٓا۟ إِلَيْهِمْ عَهْدَهُمْ إِلَىٰ مُدَّتِهِمْ إِنَّ ٱللَّهَ يُحِبُّ ٱلْمُتَّقِينَ$$

...So complete the agreement with them to the appointed term; indeed Allah loves the *muttaqoon*. [At Taubah: 4]

$$فَمَا ٱسْتَقَٰمُوا۟ لَكُمْ فَٱسْتَقِيمُوا۟ لَهُمْ إِنَّ ٱللَّهَ يُحِبُّ ٱلْمُتَّقِينَ$$

...So long as they are straightforward with you, be straightforward with them; indeed Allah loves the *muttaqoon*. [At-Taubah: 7]

The meaning of *Taqwa* has proceeded, please review what was mentioned previously concerning it.

THE PATIENT

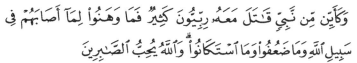

Many among the prophets fought and accompanying him (i.e, a prophet) were large numbers of religious learned men. So they weren't debilitated on account of what befell them while on the path of Allah, nor were they weakened or humbled, and Allah loves the patient. [Ali-Imran: 146]

Patience in Islam is to restrain or confine oneself as relates to three affairs. The first is to confine oneself to Allah's obedience. The second is to restrain oneself from committing disobedience to Allah, and the third is to restrain oneself from having resentment for the decree and or predetermination of Allah. The one that does this is considered to be a patient person, and Allah loves the patient as seen from the verse.

THE MUTAWAKKIL

فَإِذَا عَزَمْتَ فَتَوَكَّلْ عَلَى اللَّهِ إِنَّ اللَّهَ يُحِبُّ الْمُتَوَكِّلِينَ

...And when you've made a decision then put your trust in Allah, indeed Allah loves those who rely on Him. [Ali-Imran: 159]

The *mutawakkil* is he who practices *tawakkul* and that is being dependent on Allah and entrusting the affairs to Him;

> It is a condition specific to the heart stemming from its awareness of Allah and faith in His unique/singular standing with the creation, governance, benefit, and harm. Thus made obligatory is reliance on Him and entrusting the affairs to Him accompanied with tranquility and confidence in Him. Also certainty in His competence as relates to what you have dependency and trust in him fulfilling.[191]

---

191. Encyclopedia of Aqeedah.

THE OBJECTIVELY FAIR

وَإِنْ حَكَمْتَ فَاحْكُم بَيْنَهُم بِالْقِسْطِ إِنَّ اللَّهَ يُحِبُّ الْمُقْسِطِينَ

...And if you judge, then judge between them objectively, indeed Allah loves the objectively fair. [Al-Ma'idah: 42]

وَإِن طَائِفَتَانِ مِنَ الْمُؤْمِنِينَ اقْتَتَلُوا فَأَصْلِحُوا بَيْنَهُمَا فَإِنْ بَغَتْ إِحْدَاهُمَا عَلَى الْأُخْرَىٰ فَقَاتِلُوا الَّتِي تَبْغِي حَتَّىٰ تَفِيءَ إِلَىٰ أَمْرِ اللَّهِ فَإِن فَاءَتْ فَأَصْلِحُوا بَيْنَهُمَا بِالْعَدْلِ وَأَقْسِطُوا إِنَّ اللَّهَ يُحِبُّ الْمُقْسِطِينَ

And if two groups among the believers fall into infighting, then make reconciliation between them. However, if one among the two transgresses against the other, then all of you fight the transgressing group until it returns to the command of Allah. If it returns, make peace between the two justly and objectively; undoubtedly Allah loves the objectively fair. [Al-Hujurat: 9]

لَّا يَنْهَاكُمُ اللَّهُ عَنِ الَّذِينَ لَمْ يُقَاتِلُوكُمْ فِي الدِّينِ وَلَمْ يُخْرِجُوكُم مِّن دِيَارِكُمْ أَن تَبَرُّوهُمْ وَتُقْسِطُوا إِلَيْهِمْ إِنَّ اللَّهَ يُحِبُّ الْمُقْسِطِينَ

Allah does not forbid you from acting kindly and objectively fair with those who did not fight you on account of religion nor expelled you from your homes. Certainly Allah loves the objectively fair." [Al-Mumtahanah: 8]

CONFORMITY TO THE SUNNAH IS PROOF OF ONE'S LOVE FOR ALLAH AND MERITS ALLAH'S LOVE FOR THE SERVANT

قُلْ إِن كُنتُمْ تُحِبُّونَ اللَّهَ فَاتَّبِعُونِي يُحْبِبْكُمُ اللَّهُ وَيَغْفِرْ لَكُمْ ذُنُوبَكُمْ وَاللَّهُ غَفُورٌ رَّحِيمٌ

Say: If you really love Allah then follow me, as a result Allah will love you and forgive you for your sins and Allah is Oft-Forgiving, Mercifully Acting. [Ali-Imran: 31]

Sheikh-ul-Islam ibn Taymiyyah said while commenting on the verse: "So He made the servant's love for his Lord a motive to follow the Messenger, and made conformity to the Messenger a means to Allah's love of His servant."[192]

He also said: "Allah the glorified ordered us to follow the Messenger ﷺ and to obey, support, and love him. Also that Allah and His Messenger are more beloved to us than anyone else besides them. Consequently, He has guaranteed for us, on account of obeying and loving Him, Allah's love and generosity."[193] Additionally his statement: "So Allah's love for them results after their following of the Messenger."[194] Moreover he said: "This clarifies the fact that His love for His servant only results after the servant comes with the beloved to Him."[195]

Likewise his speech:

Actualization of the testimony that Muhammad is Allah's Messenger necessitates that obedience to him ﷺ is obedience to Allah, pleasing him is pleasing Allah, and the religion of Allah is whatsoever he instructed with. Thus the lawful is whatever he made lawful. The prohibited is whatever he made prohibited as the religion is whatever he legislated. Therefore Allah demanded from he who alleges love of Him to follow the Messenger.[196]

Also: "His (i.e. The servants) love necessitates the following of the Messenger ﷺ —and following the Messenger brings about Allah's love for the servant as Allah tests the people alleging love for Him by way

---

192. Majmu' Al-Fatawa: 1/5.

193. Majmu' Al-Fatawa: 1/334.

194. Majmu' Al-Fatawa: 6/226.

195. Majmu' Al-Fatawa: 7/443.

196. Majmu' Al-Fatawa: 8/338.

of it (i.e. their alleged love for Allah)."[197]

And his speech:

> Undoubtedly the Messenger ﷺ commands that which Allah loves and prohibits what He hates. Likewise he does what Allah loves, and he informs/notifies about what Allah loves as confirmation of it. Hence, whoever (allegedly) loves Allah it is necessary that he follows the Messenger ﷺ, thus he affirms to be the truth as pertains to what he states (i.e. his love of Allah), he obeys him as pertains to what he commands, and emulates him as pertains to what he does. So whoever does this realistically does what Allah loves resulting in Allah loving him. Additionally, Allah has made, as relates to the people He loves, two distinguishing signs. Following the Messenger and jihad on his path. This is because jihad its reality is to exert efforts in achieving what Allah loves of faith and righteous deeds. Likewise to repel whatsoever Allah hates from disbelief, immorality, and sinfulness.[198]

In conclusion, this verse establishes a yardstick in determining the truthfulness or falsity of a person's claim to love Allah. The one who truly loves Allah seeks to obtain His love and He has made the following of the Prophet's ﷺ traditions contingent in achieving this tremendous goal. Hence he who insolently, obstinately, and rebelliously refuses to conform to the Messenger's traditions, proves himself to be a liar with regards to his claim of loving Allah. How could he truly love Allah when He clarifies in the simplest of terms how to achieve His love, yet the claimant refuses to embark upon the path to obtain it?

Sheikh Muhammad Amaan al-Jami said:

> There are two affairs that are never separated; that being faith in Allah and faith in Allah's Messenger ﷺ along with loving Allah and loving the Messenger. Two coupled affairs just as the two testimonies are coupled. For instance, if a man bears witness that there is no deity in truth except Allah then stops speaking, then this is neither sufficient nor accepted as there is no value in it unless he bears witness that Muhammad is the Messenger of Allah.[199]

---

197. Majmu' Al-Fatawa: 10/81.

198. Majmu' Al-Fatawa: 10/191.

199. Sharh Usul-us-Sittah.

The following authentic narrations also substantiate this point in the clearest of terms, they are as follows:

> *Anas ibn Malik reports Allah's Messenger ﷺ statement: "Three things if found within someone, he finds by way of these things the sweetness of faith. Whoever Allah and His Messenger are more beloved to him than anyone besides them, that he loves a man yet doesn't love him except for Allah's sake, and that he hates to revert back to disbelief after Allah saved him from it just as he hates to be flung in the fire."[200]*

> *Also reported by Anas is the following from the Prophet ﷺ: "None of you (truly) believes until I am more beloved to him than his son, his father, and all of mankind."[201]*

PROPHETIC EXAMPLES ON CONFORMITY TO THE TRADITIONS OF THE MESSENGER

> *Abdullah ibn Masud said: "Allah curses female tattoo artists and the ones who request it, also females that get their eyebrows plucked, and the women that have gaps made between their teeth for beautification; women altering Allah's creation." This—statement—reached a woman from Bani Asad referred to as Umm Yaqub resulting in her coming (to him) and saying, "It has reached me that you curse such and such a person." He replied, "And what would be with me that I not curse whomever Allah's Messenger ﷺ cursed and who is mentioned in Allah's book?!" So she said, "Certainly I have read what is between its covers and have not found within it what you say." He replied, "If you read it then you've come across it. Have you not read the statement:* **"Whatever the Messenger comes to you with, take it; and whatever he forbids abstain from it."** *She said, "Of course." So he said, "Undoubtedly he has prohibited it." she said, "Indeed I have seen your family do this!" He replied, "Go and see for yourself!" So she went and looked and did not find anything from her. So Abdullah said: "Had she been like what was said, I wouldn't have married her."[202]*

---

200. Bukhari: 16 and Muslim: 43.

201. Bukhari: 15 and Muslim: 44.

202. Bukhari: 4886 and Muslim 2125.

Jabir ibn Abdullah said: "I saw a man whose opinions the people accepted, he didn't say anything except that it was accepted. So I asked 'Who is that?' And they replied, 'That is Allah's Messenger.' I said, 'O Messenger of Allah! Upon you be peace.' He ﷺ said, 'Don't say upon you be peace, indeed that is the greeting for the dead. On the contrary say peace be upon you.' I said, 'Are you Allah's Messenger?' He said, 'I am Allah's Messenger whom you call on when harm befalls to remove it, and when a drought occurs you invoke Him and He causes vegetation to sprout. If you are in the open desert and your riding beast wanders off you invoke Him and he consequently returns it to you.' I said, 'What do you advise me with?' He said, 'Never revile anyone.' And I never reviled anyone thereafter, not a freed person, slave, camel, nor sheep. He continued, 'Do not view any good deed in a lowly manner, even if you were to communicate with your brother while having a cheerful face as that is from good. Also raise your lower garment to half the shin. If you refuse, then to the ankles and beware of dragging the lower garment (i.e. below the ankles) as that is from arrogance and Allah does not love arrogance. And if a man insults you and demeans you due to what he knows is with you (of flaw), then do not demean him due to what you know of him, he will bear the consequences for such.'"[203]

Salim ibn Abdullah ibn Umar ibn-al-Khattab said: "Abdullah ibn Umar (his father) said that he heard Allah's Messenger ﷺ say, 'Don't prevent your women from the masajid when they seek your permission to go to them.' So Bilal ibn Abdullah said, 'I swear by Allah, we will prevent them.' So Abdullah approached him and reprimanded him with a severe reprimand that I have not heard the like of previously. He said, 'I inform you about the speech of the Messenger of Allah ﷺ and you say (in reply) I swear by Allah, we will prevent them!'"[204]

These narrations demonstrate the attitude and approach the Companions had in terms of emulation and conformity to the Prophet's ﷺ traditions. No one's opinion, statement, or position in an affair was given preference over his ﷺ, on the contrary they submitted to his instructions, guidance, and directives. Likewise they held others to

---

203. Abu Dawud: 4084.

204. Bukhari and Muslim: 442.

that standard as is illustrated in the last narration when Abdullah ibn Umar scolded his son Bilal for opposing his instructions pertaining to the women going to the masjid.

REMARKABLE SPEECH CONCERNING THE WALI OF ALLAH

Concerning Allah's statement:

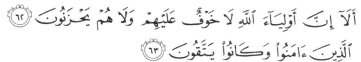

Undoubtedly the *awliyya* of Allah shall not be overcome with fear nor shall they grieve. Those who believed and exemplified taqwa. [Yunus: 62-63]

Sheikh Muhammad Amaan al-Jami made some beautiful statements regarding this verse and what it indicates concerning the *awliyya* of Allah. The following is his speech rendered into the English language:

Allah—The Glorified—via His kindness put forward the lack of fear and grief prior to defining the awliyya in order to instill a yearning within the hearts of His servants towards Him. Thereafter He states **"Those who believed and exemplified taqwa"** this is the definition of *awliyya*. The *wali* is the believer and possessor of *taqwa*, and we do not find a definition more inclusive than this definition starting with the prophets and ending with the last level (in terms of righteousness and obedience to Allah) of *awliyya*.

Furthermore, **"Those who believed"** this portion of the sentence, what enters into its meaning is whoever believed in Allah, His messengers, books, angels, the last day, His predetermination and execution (of it), and believed in everything that faith makes binding belief in, i.e. complete and perfect faith, not strictly claims to faith (i.e. that are found on the tongue but don't exist in the heart). Additionally, **"and exemplified taqwa"**: taqwa in this instance is defined as actions of the body limbs **"those who believe and do righteous deeds"** (Al-Baqarah: 25), even though the foundation is as the Prophet ﷺ stated, **"Taqwa is here"** and pointed to his chest. This correct *taqwa* is here and faith is here i.e., in the chest; however, what is in the heart of *taqwa* and faith stands in need of evidence (i.e. proving whatever claim of such to be true), and it (the evidence) is utterances of the tongue and actions of the body limbs. In other words, if guidance settles within a heart the limbs become active in worship.

When a Muslim sees within himself vigor and strong enthusiasm for worship, and desire for what is with Allah, along with lack of laziness, (instead there's) craving what is with Allah, and diligence upon obedience (to Him), then this is the meaning of guidance of the heart. The heart's guidance incites actions of the body limbs. For instance, statements of the tongue by plenitude in remembering Allah the Exalted. If a person becomes abundant in remembering Allah at every moment, i.e. while he walks, sits among people, while he's alone and no one hears him except Allah; likewise he becomes plentiful in reciting the Quran with reflection and comprehension, and in sending salutations upon the Prophet ﷺ, plentiful in invocation and humility towards Allah at every moment, then these actions indicate truthfulness concerning the faith of the heart of the claimant.

So plentifulness in remembering Allah is evidence for love and exaltation (of Him), then there are actions of the body limbs. For example, vitality in worshiping Allah as pertains to the prayer i.e., performing it in congregation as relates to the men, fasting the obligatory and voluntary fasts, spending wealth, acting mercifully, these are actions that indicate the truthfulness of a person's faith and that he has hope for what is with Allah (of favors, bounties, mercy, etc) the Glorified and Exalted.[205]

And Allah knows best. May Allah bless us to be among his sincere supporters, allies, and those beloved to Him.

---

205. Sharh Usul-us-Sittah.

The Sixth Principle

Repelling the specious arguments devised by the Shaitan as relates to abandonment of the Quran and Sunnah, along with conformity towards differing opinions and desires. This specious argument is that the Quran and Sunnah are not known (i.e. comprehended) by anyone except a mujtahid mutlaq, who is described with traits that may not be found even with (figures such as) Abu Bakr and Umar.

Hence if a person does not match this criteria, then he is required to shun the Book and Sunnah compulsorily and there is neither doubt nor ambiguity in this regard (i.e. according to this false argument). In contrast to whomever seeks guidance from these two sources, as he—consequently is viewed as—a heretic or someone mentally challenged, on account of extreme difficulty in comprehending these two textual sources (per this argument/doubt).

SubhaanAllah wa bihamdihi; how many times has Allah elucidated (His) repelling of such accursed arguments from varying perspectives i.e. legislatively, by predetermination (aspects of such overtly predictable to man), by—keen observation of—the creation, and by—His divine—commandments; to the point that it reaches the boundaries of being known by necessity. Unfortunately an abundance of people are unaware.

Author

"Indeed the statement has been proven true against most of them, thus they will not believe. Certainly We have placed iron collars on their necks, reaching their chins resulting in their heads being raised. And We placed a barrier before them and behind them, and We covered them so that they cannot see. It is the same to them regardless if you warn them or not, they will not believe. You can only (effectually) warn whomsoever conforms to the remembrance (i.e. the Quran), and knowingly fears the Infinitely Merciful (i.e. Allah) while unseen. Therefore give glad tidings of forgiveness and generous rewards to such a one (bearing the aforementioned praiseworthy traits)." [Ya-Seen: 11-7]

In closing, all praise is due to Allah Lord of all that exists, and may He commend (in lofty gatherings) and grant peace upon our leader Muhammad, his family, and his companions until the day of resurrection.

Commentator

The sixth and final principle from the author concludes his treatise with an important point, that being to follow what Allah has revealed from above the seven heavens as a source of guidance for mankind. Furthermore it attacks any and all claims to abandon this by way of doubts and misconceptions aimed at diverting a person from Allah's path regardless of how much they are beautified by the Shaitan. Therefore it is incumbent upon a person to understand that his salvation is in following the text i.e., referencing it as pertains to all acts of worship and devotion that he directs to Allah; in contrast to whatever opposes it, as that which conflicts with and contradicts this is a clear and unambiguous means to his defeat.

QURANIC EVIDENCE FOR FOLLOWING THE REVELATION [I.E. THE QURAN AND SUNNAH]

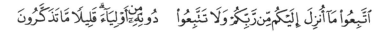

اتَّبِعُوا مَآ أُنزِلَ إِلَيْكُم مِّن رَّبِّكُمْ وَلَا تَتَّبِعُوا۟ مِن دُونِهِۦٓ أَوْلِيَآءَ قَلِيلًا مَّا تَذَكَّرُونَ

Follow what has been sent down to you by your Lord
and do not follow any allies besides Him; little is what
you remember. [Al-A'raf: 3]

قُلْ أَطِيعُوا۟ ٱللَّهَ وَٱلرَّسُولَ ۖ فَإِن تَوَلَّوْا۟ فَإِنَّ ٱللَّهَ لَا يُحِبُّ ٱلْكَٰفِرِينَ

Say: Obey Allah and the Messenger, but if they turn
away then Allah does not love the disbelievers. [Ali-
Imran: 32]

وَلَا يَأْمُرَكُمْ أَن تَتَّخِذُوا۟ ٱلْمَلَٰٓئِكَةَ وَٱلنَّبِيِّـۧنَ أَرْبَابًا ۗ أَيَأْمُرُكُم بِٱلْكُفْرِ بَعْدَ إِذْ
أَنتُم مُّسْلِمُونَ

And obey Allah and the Messenger in order to receive
mercy. [Ali-Imran: 80]

تِلْكَ حُدُودُ ٱللَّهِ ۚ وَمَن يُطِعِ ٱللَّهَ وَرَسُولَهُۥ يُدْخِلْهُ جَنَّٰتٍ
تَجْرِى مِن تَحْتِهَا ٱلْأَنْهَٰرُ خَٰلِدِينَ فِيهَا ۚ وَذَٰلِكَ ٱلْفَوْزُ
ٱلْعَظِيمُ ﴿١٣﴾ وَمَن يَعْصِ ٱللَّهَ وَرَسُولَهُۥ وَيَتَعَدَّ حُدُودَهُۥ يُدْخِلْهُ نَارًا
خَٰلِدًا فِيهَا وَلَهُۥ عَذَابٌ مُّهِينٌ ﴿١٤﴾

These are Allah's set limits, so whoever obeys Allah
and His Messenger will be admitted into paradise
underneath which rivers flow, abiding therein
forever and that is a great achievement. And whoever
disobeys Allah and His Messenger, and transgresses
His set limits; he will be entered into the fire abiding
therein forever and for him is a disgraceful torment.
[An-Nisa: 13-14]

يَٰٓأَيُّهَا ٱلَّذِينَ ءَامَنُوٓا۟ أَطِيعُوا۟ ٱللَّهَ وَأَطِيعُوا۟ ٱلرَّسُولَ وَأُو۟لِى ٱلْأَمْرِ مِنكُمْ ۖ فَإِن
تَنَٰزَعْتُمْ فِى شَىْءٍ فَرُدُّوهُ إِلَى ٱللَّهِ وَٱلرَّسُولِ إِن كُنتُمْ تُؤْمِنُونَ بِٱللَّهِ وَٱلْيَوْمِ ٱلْءَاخِرِ ۚ
ذَٰلِكَ خَيْرٌ وَأَحْسَنُ تَأْوِيلًا

O you who believe! Obey Allah and obey the Messenger
and those in authority over you, but if you differ in an
affair then refer it back to Allah and the Messenger if
you believe in Allah and the Last Day that is best and

more excellent in terms of interpretation. [An-Nisa: 59]

فَلَا وَرَبِّكَ لَا يُؤْمِنُونَ حَتَّىٰ يُحَكِّمُوكَ فِيمَا شَجَرَ بَيْنَهُمْ ثُمَّ لَا يَجِدُوا۟ فِىٓ أَنفُسِهِمْ حَرَجًا مِّمَّا قَضَيْتَ وَيُسَلِّمُوا۟ تَسْلِيمًا

So no, by your Lord, they do not believe unless they make you (i.e. Muhammad) a judge between them in disputes, and do not find subsequent to that any difficulty in your decision but submit with full submission. [An-Nisa: 65]

مَّن يُطِعِ ٱلرَّسُولَ فَقَدْ أَطَاعَ ٱللَّهَ وَمَن تَوَلَّىٰ فَمَآ أَرْسَلْنَٰكَ عَلَيْهِمْ حَفِيظًا

Whoever obeys the Messenger undoubtedly has obeyed Allah... [An-Nisa: 80]

وَأَطِيعُوا۟ ٱللَّهَ وَأَطِيعُوا۟ ٱلرَّسُولَ وَٱحْذَرُوا۟ فَإِن تَوَلَّيْتُمْ فَٱعْلَمُوٓا۟ أَنَّمَا عَلَىٰ رَسُولِنَا ٱلْبَلَٰغُ ٱلْمُبِينُ

And obey Allah and obey the Messenger, and be cautious. However, if you all turn away then know that the only duty upon Our Messenger is the clear conveyance. [Al-Maidah: 92]

يَٰٓأَيُّهَا ٱلَّذِينَ ءَامَنُوا۟ ٱسْتَجِيبُوا۟ لِلَّهِ وَلِلرَّسُولِ إِذَا دَعَاكُمْ لِمَا يُحْيِيكُمْ

O you who believe! Respond to Allah and The Messenger when He calls you to what will enliven you... [Al-Anfal: 24]

وَأَطِيعُوا۟ ٱللَّهَ وَرَسُولَهُۥ وَلَا تَنَٰزَعُوا۟ فَتَفْشَلُوا۟ وَتَذْهَبَ رِيحُكُمْ وَٱصْبِرُوٓا۟ إِنَّ ٱللَّهَ مَعَ ٱلصَّٰبِرِينَ

Obey Allah and His Messenger, and do not be at variance with one another lest you become emasculated and your strength departds. Be patient, undoubtedly

Allah is with the patient. [Al-Anfal: 46]

$$\text{إِنَّمَا كَانَ قَوْلَ ٱلْمُؤْمِنِينَ إِذَا دُعُوٓا۟ إِلَى ٱللَّهِ وَرَسُولِهِۦ لِيَحْكُمَ بَيْنَهُمْ أَن يَقُولُوا۟}$$
$$\text{سَمِعْنَا وَأَطَعْنَا ۚ وَأُو۟لَـٰٓئِكَ هُمُ ٱلْمُفْلِحُونَ ۝ وَمَن يُطِعِ ٱللَّهَ وَرَسُولَهُۥ}$$
$$\text{وَيَخْشَ ٱللَّهَ وَيَتَّقْهِ فَأُو۟لَـٰٓئِكَ هُمُ ٱلْفَآئِزُونَ ۝}$$

The only speech of the believers when they are called to Allah and His Messenger to judge between them is that they say 'we hear and obey' as they are those successful. And whoever obeys Allah and His Messenger, fears Allah, and is cautious of Him; consequently they are those successful. [An-Nur: 51-52]

$$\text{قُلْ أَطِيعُوا۟ ٱللَّهَ وَأَطِيعُوا۟ ٱلرَّسُولَ ۖ فَإِن تَوَلَّوْا۟ فَإِنَّمَا عَلَيْهِ مَا حُمِّلَ وَعَلَيْكُم}$$
$$\text{مَّا حُمِّلْتُمْ ۖ وَإِن تُطِيعُوهُ تَهْتَدُوا۟ ۚ وَمَا عَلَى ٱلرَّسُولِ إِلَّا ٱلْبَلَـٰغُ ٱلْمُبِينُ}$$

Say! Obey Allah and obey the Messenger, but if they turn away the only thing against him is what he carried and against you is what you carried; but if you obey him you are guided as there is nothing binding upon the Messenger except the clear conveyance. [An-Nur: 54]

$$\text{وَأَقِيمُوا۟ ٱلصَّلَوٰةَ وَءَاتُوا۟ ٱلزَّكَوٰةَ وَأَطِيعُوا۟ ٱلرَّسُولَ لَعَلَّكُمْ تُرْحَمُونَ}$$

And establish the prayers, pay the zakat, and obey the Messenger in order to receive mercy. [An-Nur: 56]

$$\text{وَمَا كَانَ لِمُؤْمِنٍ وَلَا مُؤْمِنَةٍ إِذَا قَضَى ٱللَّهُ وَرَسُولُهُۥٓ أَمْرًا أَن يَكُونَ لَهُمُ}$$
$$\text{ٱلْخِيَرَةُ مِنْ أَمْرِهِمْ ۗ وَمَن يَعْصِ ٱللَّهَ وَرَسُولَهُۥ فَقَدْ ضَلَّ ضَلَـٰلًا مُّبِينًا}$$

And it is not for a believing man nor woman to have a choice -for them- in their affair, if Allah and His Messenger have made a decision (i.e. in that affair). And whoever disobeys Allah and His Messenger certainly he has deviated in manifest terms. [Al-Ahzab: 36]

يُصۡلِحۡ لَكُمۡ أَعۡمَٰلَكُمۡ وَيَغۡفِرۡ لَكُمۡ ذُنُوبَكُمۡۗ وَمَن يُطِعِ ٱللَّهَ وَرَسُولَهُۥ فَقَدۡ
فَازَ فَوۡزًا عَظِيمًا

And whoever obeys Allah and His Messenger has
achieved a tremendous achievement. [Al-Ahzab: 71]

يَٰٓأَيُّهَا ٱلَّذِينَ ءَامَنُوٓاْ أَطِيعُواْ ٱللَّهَ وَأَطِيعُواْ ٱلرَّسُولَ وَلَا تُبۡطِلُوٓاْ أَعۡمَٰلَكُمۡ

O you who believe! Obey Allah and obey the Messenger,
and do not invalidate your deeds. [Muhammad: 33]

لَّيۡسَ عَلَى ٱلۡأَعۡمَىٰ حَرَجٌ وَلَا عَلَى ٱلۡأَعۡرَجِ حَرَجٌ وَلَا عَلَى ٱلۡمَرِيضِ حَرَجٌۗ وَمَن
يُطِعِ ٱللَّهَ وَرَسُولَهُۥ يُدۡخِلۡهُ جَنَّٰتٍ تَجۡرِي مِن تَحۡتِهَا ٱلۡأَنۡهَٰرُۖ وَمَن يَتَوَلَّ يُعَذِّبۡهُ
عَذَابًا أَلِيمًا

And whoever obeys Allah and His Messenger, He will
enter him into paradise underneath which rivers
flow; and whoever turns away He will punish him with
a severe punishment. [Al-Fath: 17]

إِلَّا بَلَٰغًا مِّنَ ٱللَّهِ وَرِسَٰلَٰتِهِۦۚ وَمَن يَعۡصِ ٱللَّهَ وَرَسُولَهُۥ فَإِنَّ لَهُۥ نَارَ
جَهَنَّمَ خَٰلِدِينَ فِيهَآ أَبَدًا

And whoever disobeys Allah and His Messenger
then for him is the fire of jahannam, abiding therein
forever. [Al-Jinn: 23]

These are some of the clearest evidence supporting the fact that following revelation is made binding upon everyone, and no person is exempt from this based on claims of extreme difficulty with respect to understanding the text and what it implies. As a claim of this nature conflicts with Allah's speech concerning His revelation. Allah mentions it being easy to comprehend and memorize, coupled with the fact that it was revealed in plain and simple Arabic; and there is no person more truthful in speech than Him. This point is illustrated in the following verse:

وَلَقَدۡ يَسَّرۡنَا ٱلۡقُرۡءَانَ لِلذِّكۡرِ فَهَلۡ مِن مُّدَّكِرٍ

Undoubtedly We made the Quran easy with respect to *dhikr*, so is there anyone who will remember?! [Al-Qamar: 17]

The scholars of exegesis, past and present, clarify that dhikr here refers to both remembrance and comprehension. In other words, Allah made its intent and retention easy, plain, and simple for all people. Ibn Kathir said (i.e. in his tafsir), while commenting on the verse: "Meaning; We have made its utterance easy and facilitated its intent for whoever desires it in order for the people to remember." Likewise he said about the portion of the verse {So is there anyone who will remember}, "i.e., is there anyone who will remember this Quran that which Allah has made easy its memorization and comprehension." Furthermore, there are other verses that illustrate its wordings and usage being in plain Arabic, and that it clarifies all things, as is mentioned in the following verses:

إِنَّا أَنزَلۡنَٰهُ قُرۡءَٰنًا عَرَبِيًّا لَّعَلَّكُمۡ تَعۡقِلُونَ

Indeed, We sent it down as an Arabic Quran in order for you to understand. [Yusuf: 2]

كِتَٰبٌ فُصِّلَتۡ ءَايَٰتُهُۥ قُرۡءَانًا عَرَبِيًّا لِّقَوۡمٍ يَعۡلَمُونَ

A book whose verses are detailed, an Arabic Quran for people who know. [Fussilat: 3]

إِنَّا جَعَلۡنَٰهُ قُرۡءَٰنًا عَرَبِيًّا لَّعَلَّكُمۡ تَعۡقِلُونَ

Certainly, We made it an Arabic Quran in order for you to understand." [Az-Zukhruf: 3]

وَنَزَّلۡنَا عَلَيۡكَ ٱلۡكِتَٰبَ تِبۡيَٰنًا لِّكُلِّ شَيۡءٍ وَهُدًى وَرَحۡمَةً وَبُشۡرَىٰ لِلۡمُسۡلِمِينَ

...and We have sent down to you the book making clear all things; guidance, mercy, and glad tidings for those who submit. [An-Nahl: 89]

This establishes the fact that allegations concerning the general peoples' inability to comprehend the text are categorically false, and there is no doubt in that regard. Thus the person who would persist in spreading a claim of this nature cannot be understood to be anything other than a liar and one who leads others astray advertently or inadvertently, and Allah knows best.

AUTHENTIC NARRATIONS FOR FOLLOWING THE REVELATION

Abu Huraira stated that Allah's Messenger ﷺ said: "All of my nation will enter paradise except those who refuse." They (witnesses to the statement) said: "O Messenger of Allah; who refuses?" He ﷺ said: "Whoever obeys me enters paradise, and whoever disobeys me refuses." [206]

Abu Huraira (also) narrated the Prophet's ﷺ speech: "Whoever obeys me, undoubtedly he has obeyed Allah. Whoever disobeys me, certainly he disobeys Allah. In addition, whoever obeys the leader has obeyed me, and whoever disobeys the leader has disobeyed me." [207]

Jabir ibn Abdullah said: "Angels came to the Prophet ﷺ while he was sleeping resulting in some of them saying, 'Indeed he is asleep.' Others among them said, 'Surely his eyes are asleep but his heart is awake.' And then said, 'For this comrade of yours there is a similitude, so put forth for him the similitude!' So some said, 'He's asleep.' While others said, 'His eyes are asleep but his heart is awake.' Thus they said, 'His similitude is identical to a man who built a house, prepared a banquet therein, and sent out an inviter (to the banquet). So whoever responded to the invitation entered the home and partook in the banquet; in contrast to whoever did not accept the invitation, as he didn't enter the home nor did he partake in the banquet.' So some (of the angels) said, 'interpret it for him.' Some said, 'He's asleep.' Others said, 'His eyes are asleep, but his heart is wide awake.' So they said, 'The home signifies paradise

---

206. Bukhari: 7280.

207. Bukhari: 7137 and Muslim: 1835.

and the inviter is Muhammad. Thus whoever obeys Muhammad, obeys Allah; and whoever disobeys Muhammad has disobeyed Allah. Also Muhammad makes distinction between the people."* [208]*

Abu Musa al-Ash'ari narrated the Prophet's ﷺ speech: "My example and the example of that which I have been sent with is like a man who comes to a people and says, 'O people! Indeed I have seen an army with my two eyes, and undoubtedly I am a naked warner in order for (your) salvation. Consequently a group among the people obeyed him. They headed out after nightfall moving leisurely until they were saved. In contrast, a group denied and remained in their place til morning. Thus the army invaded during the morning hours and annihilated them. Hence, this is the example of whoever obeys me and follows what I have been sent with (i.e. revelation). Likewise it's an example of whoever disobeys me and denies what I have been sent with, of truth."[209]

Abu Huraira quotes Allah's Messenger ﷺ as saying: "By Him in whose hand is Muhammad's soul, no one from this nation hears of me whether he be Jew or Christian then dies without believing in what I was sent with except that he is among the inhabitants of the fire."[210]

Anas ibn Malik said: "A contingent among the Prophet's ﷺ companions asked his wives about his private actions. As a result some said, 'I will not marry women.' Others said, 'I will not eat meat.' and another said, 'I will not sleep during the night.' Consequently the Prophet praised Allah and then said, 'What is with the people that said such-and-such?! Rather I pray and sleep, I fast and break my fast, and I marry women; thus whoever has disdain for my Sunnah is not from me.'"[211]

Abu Huraira said that the Prophet ﷺ said: "There isn't a prophet among the prophets except that he was given from miracles what is similar to it (i.e, from miracles given to other prophets), on account of

---

208. Bukhari: 7281.

209. Bukhari: 7283 and Muslim 2283.

210. Muslim: 153.

211. Bukhari: 5063 and Muslim: 1401.

which the people were secure (i.e. in faith). Additionally what was given to me is only revelation Allah revealed to me. Therefore, I hope I am most abundant in being followed on the day of resurrection."[212]

Al-Miqdam ibn Mudi Karib said that Allah's Messenger صَلَّى ٱللَّهُ عَلَيْهِ وَسَلَّمَ *said: "Alas I've been given the book and its like along with it, yet we are on the verge (of a time period) where a full bellied man will be reclining on his couch saying, 'Upon you is this Quran, thus whatever you find within it of lawful matters, declare it lawful; and whatever you find within it of prohibited matters, declare it prohibited.' Nonetheless, the domesticated donkey is not permissible. Neither is any beast of prey with fangs, nor any lost item of a confederate, unless its owner has no need of it. Whoever comes upon a people, then it is incumbent that they entertain him; however, if they do not entertain him then he is to act with them in the same manner of his treatment (i.e. from them)."*[213]

Abu Rafi mentioned that the Prophet صَلَّى ٱللَّهُ عَلَيْهِ وَسَلَّمَ *said: "Do not let me find any of you reclining on his cushion while a command from my commands, whether it be what I ordered or forbade, comes to him and then he says, 'I have no idea, we didn't find it in Allah's book as we (only) follow it.'"*[214]

Urwah said that Az-Zubayr had an argument with a man from the Ansar over a gully in a stony area resulting in the Prophet صَلَّى ٱللَّهُ عَلَيْهِ وَسَلَّمَ *saying: "O Az-Zubayr! Irrigate then send (i.e. allow to flow) the water to your neighbor." Consequently, the Ansari said: "O Messenger of Allah! It (i.e. the decision) is because he is your cousin." Thus the face of the Prophet* صَلَّى ٱللَّهُ عَلَيْهِ وَسَلَّمَ *changed in temperament and he said: "Irrigate O Az-Zubayr, then restrict the water until it returns to the wall and at that point allow it to flow to your neighbor." The Prophet* صَلَّى ٱللَّهُ عَلَيْهِ وَسَلَّمَ *gave Az-Zubayr his full right in an unambiguous ruling after the Ansari angered him, prior to that he gave an order favorable to both of them. Az-Zubayr said: "I don't believe that this verse was revealed except on account of that* **'So no, by your Lord, they do not believe unless they make you a**

---

212. Bukhari: 4981 and Muslim: 152.

213. Abu Dawud: 4604 and Ibn Majah: 12.

214. Abu Dawud: 4605 and Ibn Majah: 13.

judge between them in disputes."[215]

Abdullah ibn Masud said: "Allah curses the female tattooer and the woman who requests a tattoo, The woman who plucks her eyebrows, The female who makes gaps between the teeth for beautification, i.e. modifiers to Allah's creation." So this reached a woman from Bani Sa'ad titled Um-Yaqub, she came and said, "It has reached me that you curse this type of person?" He replied, "And what is with me that I should not curse who Allah's Messenger ﷺ cursed, and who is mentioned in Allah's Book?" She said, "Undoubtedly I have read what is between its covers (i.e. in its entirety) and have not found within it what you say." He stated, "If you read it you would have stumbled upon it. Did you not read: {And whatever the Messenger comes with, then take it; and whatever he prohibits, then abstain from it}? She responded, "Of course!" Thus he said, "Surely he ﷺ prohibited it." She said, "Indeed I saw your family doing this." He replied, "Then go to them and examine (thoroughly)." So she went and looked and did not see anything from her eyebrows of this nature (i.e. plucking). Ibn Masud then said, "If her situation was like that I would not keep company with her."[216]

ADHERENCE TO REVELATION IS THE MEANS TO SALVATION

Oftentimes we hear within our society argumentation designed to divert people away from what Allah has revealed of guidance. Arguments such as, "Man inherently knows right from wrong" or "Man is capable of distinguishing right from wrong" all in an attempt to disqualify the worth of the revealed books and the wisdom for which they were revealed. These arguments and those that stem from them are meant to insult the intelligence of the adherent to revelation, shame him/her for their alleged lack of competency, and assert the intellectual dominance of the person presenting such arguments along with their lack of need to submit to revelation.

---

215. Bukhari: 2360 and 4585.

216. Bukhari: 4886 and Muslim: 2125.

Although this particular argument has some merit to a small degree, the annals of human history prove otherwise in the preponderant sense of what these arguments entail. Within the history of humanity you have brutal atrocities that have taken place, some being embedded within the cultures of people. For instance, the trans Atlantic slave trade is an example of how barbaric, evil, and inhumane the descendants of Adam can become, as the horrors committed by Europeans against African slaves are from the most savage of acts within recent world history that dispel the arguments of the rejectors of revelation. In fact, these atrocities were committed by people who allegedly followed a book that clearly didn't condone chattel slavery, yet look how far they stomped. Where was their distinction between right and wrong for that 250 year period? This is just one example out of many atrocities within human history.

Additionally, revelation does not only consist of laws, i.e. commands and prohibitions. On the contrary, revelation consists of more than that to help shape the thought and world view of its adherents, to have them comprehend the reality of this world and their purpose in it, to soften their hearts as relates to the Creator and His divinity by detailing who He is, and to keep them focused on the ultimate goal. Ibn Qayyim al-Jawziyya said concerning the Quran:

> The majority of the chapters of the Quran, on the contrary all of the chapters of the Quran are inclusive of the two types of tawheed. Rather, we say a complete statement that every verse within the Quran is inclusive of tawheed, an evidence to it, and a caller towards it. Thus the Quran -at times- it is a notification about Allah; His names, attributes, and actions; this is the knowledge related informational aspect of tawheed. Or it calls towards His worship alone without any partners along with forgoing all of what is worshiped besides Him, and this is the intention and request related tawheed. As for commands, prohibitions, obliging with obedience to Him; these are the rights of tawheed and what completes it. Furthermore it's a notification about His generosity towards the adherents of tawheed and His obedience, also how He interacted with them in this worldly life and how He will honor them in the next life; this is the rewards of tawheed. Likewise it is a notification about the idolaters and how He acted with them in this worldly life from exemplary punishment and what He will cause to happen to them in the end from torment; this is the recompense for whoever exits from

the rulings of tawheed.[217]

This is an excellent and well rounded explanation of what the revelation includes that further clarifies the ignorance of these arguments. Moreover Sheikh-ul-Islam ibn Taymiyyah has some beautiful statements which illustrate the value of revelation and its importance in the life of the child of Adam, as it is essential for his salvation. The following are some of his speech:

> Faith in prophecy/prophethood is the foundation for salvation and bliss. Thus, whoever does not actualize this affair, confusion overcomes him as relates to the issue of guidance and deviation, faith and disbelief, and he does not distinguish between error and the correct.[218]

A beneficial principle as pertains to the obligation of adherence to revelation along with a clarification that happiness and guidance is in conformity to the Messenger ﷺ (i.e. his teachings), as opposed to misguidance and misery being in opposition to it. Also that every good in existence, whether general or specific, stems from the direction of the Messenger; in contrast to every evil in the world particularized to the servant, as its cause is contention to the Messenger or ignorance to that with which he came. In addition, that the happiness of the servant as relates to his worldly existence and his life in the next is contingent upon following the message.

Messengership/revelation is essential for the servants, their need for it exceeds their need for anything else. Moreover, messengership/revelation is the soul of the worldly existence and its light and life, so is there any rectification for the worldly life if its soul, light, and life are absent?! The world is dark and cursed except the portion in which the sun of messengership rises over. Similarly, the servant is in darkness and is among the dead until the sun of messengership peaks within his heart (bringing light), nourishing his life and soul. Allah says: **"Or is he who is dead then We enlivened him and made for him a light with which he walks among man like he who is in darkness that he can never come out?"** [Al An'am: 122]

So this is the description of the believer, he was dead in the darkness of ignorance then Allah enlivened him by usage of the soul of messengership and the light of faith. He made for him light that he

---

217. مدارج السالكين في منازل السائرين.

218. Kitab An-Nubawwat.

walked with among the people.[219]

Allah made the messengers mediums between Himself and His servants as relates to notifying them of what benefits and harms them, and in completion of their rectification as pertains to their temporal lives and their hereafter. They were sent to call to Allah and to define the path that eventually leads to Him along with clarification of their state after returning to Him.

So the first fundamental (i.e. of what the messengers clarified) includes affirmation of the qualities (i.e. of Allah), monotheism, and the predetermination. Likewise, Allah mentions the time periods related to His beloved allies and His enemies as these are the stories that He narrates to His servants. The second fundamental includes the elaboration of legislated acts, commands; prohibitions; and the allowed, and notification of what Allah loves and hates. The third is inclusive of belief in the hereafter, paradise and the fire, and rewards and punishment.

Thus, around these three fundamentals revolves the creation and the command, and happiness and success are granted on account of it. In addition, there is no path towards understanding these affairs except through the messengers as the intellect cannot guide towards its detailed aspects nor awareness of its true realities, although it may perceive the surface requirement for it in general. Similar to a patient that perceives the need for medicine and he who administers such; however, this perception cannot guide him to the detailed aspects of the ailment or usage of the proper medication against it. Nonetheless, the servant's need for revelation is greater than the patient's need for medication as the last stage of what occurs as a result of lack of a doctor is the death of the body, whereas if the servant doesn't acquire the light of revelation and its life his heart dies a death in which life is never expected to accompany him thereafter ever.[220]

Revelation is essential for the rectification of the servant as it pertains to his worldly affairs and his hereafter. So, just like there is no rectification for him as pertains to his hereafter except by following the revelation, then there also is not for him any rectification as pertains to his worldly affairs except by following the revelation; hence, the person is compelled to enact the Islamic Legislation consequently standing between two procedural moves. The procedural move by

---

219. Majmu' Al-Fatawa: 19/94.

220. Majmu' Al-Fatawa: 19/96-97.

which he obtains what benefits him and the procedural move by which he repels what harms him. The Islamic Legislation (i.e. revelation) is light that clarifies what benefits from what harms, it is Allah's light within the earth, His justice between His servants, and His fortress that any who enters is (consequently) safe.

Furthermore, what is not intended by the Islamic legislation is the distinction between the harmful and the beneficial by way of senses as that is achieved even with undomesticated animals. Surely the donkey and camel can distinguish between barley and dirt. On the contrary, the distinction is between actions that harm its implementer in this life and the hereafter. For example, the benefit of faith and monotheism, justice and righteousness, charity and good deeds, integrity and virtue, bravery and tolerance, patience while enjoining good and forbidding evil, maintaining family ties and dutifulness to parents, treating the slaves and neighbors in a good manner, fulfillment of rights, sincerity of actions for Allah's sake and dependency upon Him, seeking assistance from Him and contentment as relates to the occurrences predetermined by Him, submission to His judgments and willful compliance to His commands, loving His beloved allies and enmity for His enemies, knowledge related fear of him in private and public, fear of Him resulting in performance of obligatory acts and avoiding the prohibited, expectation of the rewards with Him, affirming to be the truth that which He and His messengers report, obedience to Him in everything they command from what is beneficial and profitable to the servant in this worldly life and in the hereafter. In contrast to what is opposite to that of misfortune and harm as pertains to the servant's worldly life and the hereafter.

Therefore, if there was no revelation the intellect would not be able to guide towards the details of the beneficial and harmful as relates to worldly existence and the hereafter since the greatest blessing of Allah bestowed upon His servants and the most honorable bounty given to them is that He sent to them messengers, revealed to them the books, and made explicitly clear to them the straight path. If it wasn't for that they would be on the level of cattle and livestock, on the contrary in a worse condition than that. Conversely, whoever accepts Allah's revelation and is upright in implementation of it then he is from the best of creation; however, he who rejects it accordingly is among the worst of creation and is upon the worst of conditions more so than the dog, pig, and four legged animals.[221]

All praises are for Allah alone He who sent a messenger to us from

---

221. Majmu' Al-Fatawa: 19/99.

among us reciting to us Allah's verses, purifying us, and teaching us the book and the wisdom, although prior to that we were in manifest misguidance. The inhabitants of paradise will say: **"All praises are for Allah Who guided us to this and if it were not for Allah guiding us we would not have been guided. Undoubtedly the messengers of our Lord came with the truth"** [Al-A'raf: 43]. In brief, the worldly life is cursed, whatever is within it is cursed except that which the sun of revelation rises upon and he whose building is erected upon it. So nothing remains for the people of the earth as long as the impact of the messengers exist within them. Thus if the traces of the messengers were completely wiped away from the earth then Allah would destroy the upper and lower aspects of existence and usher in the resurrection.

The need of the inhabitants of the earth for the messenger is not like their need for the sun and the moon, nor the wind and rain. It is not like man's need for life, or the eye's need for light, or the body's need for food and drink. On the contrary it is greater than these things and is a more severe need than all of what he is capable (i.e. to obtain) and or what he could imagine. Hence, the messengers are a medium between Allah and His creation as it pertains to His commands and prohibitions as they are the ambassadors between Him and His servants. Muhammad ibn Abdullah, who was the last of them, their leading figure, and most honored with his Lord, said: "O mankind! I have only been sent as a gifted mercy." Likewise Allah says **"And We have not sent you except as a mercy for mankind"** [Al-Anbiya: 107].

Additionally, he ﷺ said: "Undoubtedly Allah looked at the people of the earth i.e., the Arab and non Arab, and severely hated them except a small portion among the people of the scripture." This hatred was on account of their lack of guidance provided by the messengers, subsequently Allah removed this hatred by way of the Messenger ﷺ as he sent him as a mercy to mankind, an aspiration for the righteous, and a proof for all of creation. Allah prescribed for His servants obedience, love, support, and veneration of him along with fulfillment of his rights, and channeling all paths towards him. As a result no path should be opened to anyone unless it is his path as all prophets and messengers made a covenant to have faith in and follow him, and Allah commanded them to make this covenant with whoever followed them among the believers.

Primarily, Allah sent him with guidance and the religion of truth as a giver of glad tidings and a warner before the establishment of the Hour. Furthermore, He ﷺ is a caller to Allah by His permission, a guiding light, and finality of messengership. Allah uses him to guide away from deviance, to teach against ignorance, to revive the sight of the blind on account of his messengership, to grant hearing to the deaf, and to closed hearts. Emphatically, He illuminated the earth by way of his ﷺ messengership after its darkness, united the hearts by way of it after their splitting, straightened (i.e. made correct or put in order) by way of it all crooked doctrines, and made explicitly clear by usage of it unequivocal proofs.

Moreover -as relates to the Messenger- Allah placed the joy of acceptance within his heart, removed his sins, raised his mention (throughout the earth), and prescribed defeat and humiliation on whoever opposes him. Allah sent Muhammad ﷺ at a time during a break in revelation and messengership. Likewise at a time of learning the books whilst they had been distorted, the legislations changed, and the most oppressive of opinions were what the people clung to. They would make rulings about Allah and between His servants with corrupt statements and their desires. Therefore, Allah guided the entire creation by way of him, made clear the straight path due to him, and extracted the people from the various darknesses into the (one) light. He gave sight to the blind, and guided away from deviation by means of him. He made him ﷺ a dividing factor between Paradise and Hell, a separator of the righteous from the unrighteous, and made the guidance and success as a result of conformity to him and acting accordingly with him. In contrast to misguidance and misfortune resulting from disobedience and opposition to him.[222]

All praises are due to Allah who has made sufficient this speech of Sheikh-ul-Islam in illustrating this important point. This concludes commentary to this momentous work and I ask Allah to reward its author immensely and continue to allow it to be an ongoing charity for him. Lastly, may Allah's lofty commendations and peace be upon our Messenger Muhammad, his family, and all of his companions, and all praises are due to Allah alone Lord of all that exist.

---

222. Majmu' Al-Fatawa: 19/101-102.

NOTES

NOTES

NOTES

NOTES

NOTES

Made in the USA
Middletown, DE
11 September 2024

60099721R00109